what people are saying about
• living for a single purpose •

"Most of us have discovered that the twists and turns of life often take us to places we never expected to visit, much less, stay. In their compelling book, *Living for a Single Purpose*, authors Adessa Holden and Jennie Puleo show us that singleness need not be a parched desert where one just hopes to survive, but a green garden where purpose thrives and tendrils of beauty lace the landscape. Whether you are single, married, or single again due to death or divorce, the raw honesty, warm humor, practical wisdom, and spiritual encouragement in this book will inspire you to trust in God's greater purposes for your own twists-and-turns journey!"

—**Dr. Jodi Detrick**,
speaker, leadership coach, and author of
The Jesus-Hearted Woman

"Sometimes, life is not what you expect it to be and you find yourself trapped in a season that you didn't want. *Living for a Single Purpose* will revolutionize the way you think about these different seasons of life. Adessa and Jennie teach us how to step outside the unknown and embrace the choices we have that will lead us to a life of purpose for God."

—**Angela Craig**,
director of the NWMN Women's Department, author of
Pivot Leadership: Small Steps…Big Change, and speaker

"Practical, biblical, and insightful! Adessa and Jennie capture the heart of a godly woman. *Living for a Single Purpose* sets the stage to live a life of fulfillment whether single or married. It is a must read no matter your path in life."

—**Marjie Tourville,**
wife of the superintendent of the
PennDel Ministries Network of the Assemblies of God,
and director of Women in Ministry

"Both Adessa and Jennie are honest, insightful, and practical in *Living for a Single Purpose.* Every single woman can relate to the struggles shared in this book, yet be enlightened by the spiritual application, encouraged to ask the right questions, and challenged to make wise choices. No matter what your status is right now, whether single or not, you will grow in your relationship with God if you allow the truths of this book to become a reality in your own life. They have clearly stated that we all need a single purpose by which to live and only God can give us that purpose."

—**Rev. Ruth E. Puleo,**
ordained minister and director of the Women of Purpose of
the PennDel Ministries Network of the Assemblies of God.
Served as associate pastor with her husband, and is a
writer, speaker, and missionary evangelist.

"Jennie Puleo knows what it feels like to have your life turned upside down and to end up living a life that is the opposite of all your hopes and dreams. More importantly, she has discovered the gift of turning pain into purpose. If your life hasn't gone the way you planned it, Jennie has a powerful message just for you."

—**Valorie Burton,**
bestselling author of
Successful Women Think Differently

living for a single purpose

living *for a* single purpose

adessa holden & jennie puleo
forasinglepurpose.com

MORNING JOY MEDIA
spring city, pennsylvania

Copyright © 2015 Adessa Holden and Jennie Puleo

All rights reserved. No portion of this book may be reproduced, stored in a retrieval system, or transmitted in any form or by any means—electronic, mechanical, photocopy, recording, scanning, or other—except for brief quotations in reviews or articles, without the prior written permission of the author.

Published by Morning Joy Media.

Visit www.morningjoymedia.com for more information on bulk discounts and special promotions, or e-mail your questions to info@morningjoymedia.com.

All Scripture quotations, unless otherwise indicated, are taken from the Holy Bible, New International Version®, NIV®. Copyright ©1973, 1978, 1984, 2011 by Biblica, Inc.™ Used by permission of Zondervan. All rights reserved worldwide. www.zondervan.com The "NIV" and "New International Version" are trademarks registered in the United States Patent and Trademark Office by Biblica, Inc.™

Scripture quotations marked (NLT) are taken from the Holy Bible, New Living Translation, copyright ©1996, 2004, 2007, 2013 by Tyndale House Foundation. Used by permission of Tyndale House Publishers, Inc., Carol Stream, Illinois 60188. All rights reserved.

Scripture quotations marked (ESV) are from the ESV® Bible (The Holy Bible, English Standard Version®), copyright © 2001 by Crossway, a publishing ministry of Good News Publishers. Used by permission. All rights reserved.

Scripture quotations marked (The Message) from THE MESSAGE. Copyright © by Eugene H. Peterson 1993, 1994, 1995, 1996, 2000, 2001, 2002. Used by permission of Tyndale House Publishers, Inc.

Scripture verses marked (KJV) are from the King James Version of the Bible.

Design: Debbie Capeci

Subject Headings:

1. Christian women—Religious life. 2. Christian life. I. Title.

ISBN 978-1-937107-47-5 (paperback)
ISBN 978-1-937107-48-2 (ebook)

Printed in the United States of America

I would like to dedicate this book to Jesus—the true love of my life.

Thank you for loving me, wanting me, healing me, changing me, and allowing me the privilege to serve you. Thank you for walking beside me every day of my life—through the good and bad and everything in between. Thank you for having a plan and a purpose even when I couldn't see a plan at all. It's my heart's desire that this book challenges and inspires other women to pursue a deeper, more intimate relationship with you. This book belongs to you.

I'd also like to thank my brother, Jamie, for all of his help, support, and encouragement as we went through this process. Thanks for believing in this ministry and allowing me the freedom to follow God fearlessly. It's an honor to serve God with you.

—adessa

It is apparent (especially after reading this book) that I would not be where I am or who I am without the steady and persistent presence of Jesus Christ in my life. I'm daily grateful for how he's carried me, guided me, and sustained me through the most difficult and heart-breaking circumstances I've ever known. Without him, I'd have nothing of value to write, and for that purpose, I credit him for the words penned on each page of this book.

I'm aware now, more than ever, of the people that God has strategically placed in my life to support, encourage, cheer me on, and pray for me on my journey. You have not gone unnoticed.

Natalia "Tali-girl"—there are no words to express the value of the gift that you are to me. You challenge me to be the best version of myself; to love freely and forgive often. We have walked through deep, dark waters together and I've seen you rise up and learn how to jump the waves of life with grace and beauty. I'm proud to be your mom.

Dad—you've inspired me to always strive to be the person God desires me to be and taught me that it's never too late to pursue God-given dreams. Thank you for being an amazing "Papa" and the consistent man in my and Tali's life. I will always be your "Cocoa."

Mom—my #1 fan. My prayer warrior, friend, cheerleader, and encourager; thank you for teaching me to love people unconditionally and across many borders. You are a fine example of a mother, wife, "Nana," mentor, teacher, and minister. Your passion to love and serve women in all walks of life is one that I desire to emulate.

To all the women and dear friends—you know who you are—that have steadily carried me in prayer, sat with me while I cried, and loved the messiest versions of myself: I am eternally grateful and indebted to you.

jennie

contents

introduction • 1

1 • choosing to surrender • 7

2 • choosing obedience • 19

3 • choosing the right relationship • 25

4 • choosing to forgive God • 35

5 • choosing to let go: take out the trash • 51

6 • choosing to overcome your past • 59

7 • choosing to forgive • 75

8 • choosing to overcome shame • 85

9 • choosing contentment • 101

10 • choosing to not get stuck • 113

11 • choosing true love • 123

12 • choosing to never settle • 135

13 • choosing to not be a desperate female hunter • 145

14 • choosing purity • 165

15 • choosing purity again • 185

16 • choosing to live for a single purpose • 191

conclusion • 203

about the authors • 205

• adessa

introduction

I remember it like it was yesterday. I was almost twenty-one years old and a junior in Bible college. I'd just spent another exciting Friday night babysitting two adorable little boys while a professor and his wife had a date night. Afterward, on the ride home, my professor (trying to make conversation) asked, "So what are your plans for after graduation?"

At the time, I hated that question because I didn't really have a good answer. That's humorous because a few years earlier when I started college I thought I had a foolproof plan for my life.

Go to Bible college—Meet future husband—Fall in love—Live happily ever after as a pastor's wife.

Only now there was a problem. Here I was, well into my junior year, and I wasn't dating anyone. I was big-time disappointed with God and life in general. So here I was, heartbroken and angry, being asked about my plans for the future.

That's when I spoke a sentence filled with more honesty than I'd probably admitted to myself until that time. I said, "I don't really know what I'm going to do. It doesn't seem like there are a lot of options available to me as a single woman."

Then my professor said some words that at the time seemed ludicrous, but I now see were the absolute truth that I needed to hear. He said, "What do you mean, 'there are no choices'? The whole world is available to you. This is the greatest time in your life because you can choose any life you want."

And with those words, we arrived at my dorm. He went home and I thought, *Yeah, right, what do you know?*

Now, twenty years later, I realize he knew *a lot*. In fact, he was absolutely right. I couldn't see it at the time because of tunnel vision. I wanted what I wanted, the way I wanted it, at the time I wanted it, and refused to see the possibilities beyond that one choice I'd given myself in life. The blinders I chose to wear were blocking my view of all the limitless possibilities for a rich, full life that are available to the single woman who is willing to live her life for God's purposes.

When we change our attitudes and open our eyes to all the possibilities, we see that my professor was right—the choices and possibilities are endless. This is true whether you're a young woman just venturing out in life, a more mature woman that's never been married, or a woman who's single again after losing a partner to divorce or death. Just because your life didn't turn out like the romantic fairy tale that you imagined doesn't mean your choices or opportunities to have an amazing life are over. The truth is that they may have just begun.

Recently, Jennie and I had the opportunity to speak at a ministry event for single moms. As I sat listening to the other speakers, I realized that even though we hadn't coordinated our messages or workshops beforehand, the Holy Spirit drew each of us back to the topic of *choices*. Specifically, each speaker said over and over again throughout the event: "As single women you have the chance to make choices that will reap positive results in your life. Today, you have the opportunity to say, 'Regardless of what happened in the past, today I am going to make a choice to start following the principles that God laid out in the Bible and let them direct my future.'"

While both single and married women have the power to make positive choices that lead to positive consequences in life, single women have one benefit over married women. The apostle Paul puts it this way:

> *An unmarried woman or virgin is concerned about the Lord's affairs: Her aim is to be devoted to the Lord in both body and spirit. But a married woman is concerned about the affairs of this world—how she can please her husband. I am saying this for your own good, not to restrict you, but that you may live in a right way in undivided devotion to the Lord (1 Corinthians 7:34–35).*

A married woman is restricted in the options she has in life. Her decisions need to be made in partnership with her husband, taking his preferences, his needs, and his wants into consideration. If we were really honest with ourselves, we all know married women who say, "I would love to be able to make a different choice, but my husband would never go for it." This can apply to anything from career goals to financial decisions, and even extends into whether or not a woman can fully follow and apply God's principles to her life. The truth is that a married woman is part of a team, and her choices are limited and influenced by the other members of that team.

Please do not misunderstand me. I'm not anti-marriage or pushing a pro-feminist agenda. When it is God's will that a woman be married and live her life serving God in partnership, it is a very fulfilling life. However, this book is written to single women to make a specific point.

The point is: Too often, when God allows us to experience a season of singleness in our lives, we can feel like our choices are limited because we aren't married. Looking at life through this blurred lens makes us feel as if we will never be able to live happy, fulfilled lives because of limited options.

The purpose of this book is to show you that nothing could be further from the truth. Rather than having limited choices, as a single woman, you actually have more choices and more freedom to follow whatever God's plan is for your life. Because you have fewer commitments, you are able to explore more possibilities and take more opportunities than your married counterparts.

My professor was right: "The whole world is available to you. This is the greatest time in your life because you can choose any life you want." As single women you have the chance to make choices that will reap positive results in your life.

I just wish it hadn't taken me ten years to realize he was right.

I'm thankful I did eventually come around. Sometime in my late 20s I began to understand that wishing my life was different and waiting for my prince to come wasn't leading to a fulfilled and happy life. Instead, I learned that I needed to start making the choice to lead a happy and fulfilled life *now*, as a single woman, and if things change later, great. If not, this is my life; I might as well start living it, loving it, enjoying it, and getting as much out of it as possible.

That's why this book is all about choices. In this book, Jennie and I talk about some of the choices we've made that have completely revolutionized our lives and our outlook as Christian single women. Just as my professor challenged me years ago, today we are challenging you to make these choices in your own life, and see if you don't eventually find that the possibilities for a happy, fulfilling life really are endless for the Christian single woman who decides to make right choices.

chapter 1 • adessa

choosing to surrender

All I ever really wanted in life was to be married. There—I said it.

Even as a little girl, whenever people would ask me what I wanted to be when I grew up, my answer always involved the word "wife."

Pastor's wife.

A stay-at-home mom that wrote on the side.

A counselor at my husband's church.

The possibility of being an adult single woman *never* entered my mind. (Except possibly as a worst-case scenario and we all know that God would NEVER let something that tragic happen to one of his children.)

I grew up in a small town in rural Pennsylvania where everyone married young. Those who didn't marry their high school sweethearts went away to college and came home with a husband. Anything else was abnormal. We all felt sorry for the very, very few single women that we knew. (Looking back, I remember two, and one was a missionary.)

Just before my fifth birthday, a neighbor asked my mom if she'd like to come with her to the local Pentecostal church. Being on her own search for a personal relationship with God and meaning in her life, my mom jumped at the chance. On a Sunday evening when a traveling evangelist gave an altar call, she went forward and accepted Jesus as her Savior.

That night changed everything. Mostly it changed my mom, which brought big changes to our family. I can still remember her talking about that night decades later, her eyes sparkling with the full wonder of a young girl in love. She said that night, when the evangelist picked her out of a crowd of people and asked her personally, "Do you want to have a personal relationship with God?" she knew for the first time ever that she was loved.

Among the myriad of people at the altar, God had chosen *her*. She often said she decided right then that if God wanted her that much, then from that day forward, the rest of her life was his. She was what we now call "all in." Nothing was ever the same after that special night.

A few weeks later, on another Sunday night, I asked my mom if I could go to church with her. (Okay, it was more like the begging and crying that comes when a four-year-old wants something, but she said I could go anyway.) In a few moments, I had on my best Winnie-the-Pooh Sunday dress with my patent leather Mary Janes and we were off.

I don't remember a lot about the service that night, only that the room seemed enormous and filled with people. I have no recollection of what the pastor spoke about, but it must have left an impression because following the service, I went home, crawled behind the sofa, and asked Jesus to come into my heart. Later that night, I told my mom, who talked to me about my decision and prayed with me again. Even though I was only four years old at the time, this decision was a turning point in my life. It was a very real commitment from an earnest heart that wanted to give her entire life to Jesus. That night changed everything.

Over the course of the next two years, my dad started attending church and we became a church-going Pentecostal family. My mom continued to grow in her relationship with God and continued her pattern of being "all in." She didn't just keep this relationship to herself, but she dedicated herself to passing her passion for God on to my brother and me.

She taught us to pray and read the Bible (when we could read). She initiated family devotions, took us to church, and, at great personal sacrifice, enrolled us in Christian school. Because she was so invested in feeding our spiritual lives, my relationship with God and my faith continued to grow. Even though I was a "church kid," I was also a child with a very deep and intimate relationship with Jesus. Like my mom, I was "all in."

I was seven years old when another Sunday night service changed the trajectory of my life. Yet again, there was a special speaker: a traveling team of students from Faith School of Theology, a Bible college in Maine. They sang and performed skits before one of the gentlemen came to the pulpit and spoke about the donkey that Jesus rode into Jerusalem during the triumphal entry. It was so many years ago that I don't remember all the points, but the general idea was surrendering all to Jesus so that he could accomplish his will.

At the end of the sermon, the speaker gave an altar call for anyone that wanted to answer God's call to ministry. Hearing the Holy Spirit's call, I practically ran to the altar to surrender my life to Jesus and his service. Even at seven, I meant it. From that day forward, my life belonged to Jesus. I just didn't exactly know what that meant.

You see, even though my heart and my spirit were in the right place and I did make a genuine commitment, the other side of the coin was that I was seven years old—there was no way I could fully grasp the gravity of the decision I'd made that day. In my mind, I'd gone forward to answer God's call to ministry. From the limited perspective of a seven-year-old, that meant one thing: Someday I would go off to Bible college, fall in love, get married, and my husband and I would be in full-time ministry. I mean, obviously, what else *could* it mean?

And that was my life's plan.

It was my plan as I continued growing up, going to school, going to church, and coming of age.

It continued to be my plan when I became a teenager and knew that I really only wanted to date guys with the same personal relationship with Jesus and calling to go into full-time ministry.

After I graduated from high school, I headed off to Bible college to start putting the plan into action.

Marriage and ministry, here we come! After all, that's what I'd agreed to, right?

Wrong.

As you all know, God had a different plan.

The question now became, *Was my life dedicated to following God's plan wherever it led, or was I simply dedicated to fulfilling my plan for my life?*

Tough question.

I'll be honest, it's a question I've had to answer more than once over the last twenty years.

Being even more vulnerable, I'll admit it's a question I didn't always answer correctly.

It's hard for our deepest desires to die. As humans, we are wired to be innately selfish and want what we want, doing everything we can to achieve it.

When God comes into the equation and asks, "Do you love me enough to give me your entire life, to let me lead and guide you along the paths that I have for you, whatever they may be," there is a natural tug of war inside our hearts.

Speaking from my own experience, whenever I have been confronted with this choice, there's always a part of me that wants to passionately follow God, throw caution to the wind, and say, "Wherever you go, I will go too." Of course, there's also the very human part of me that says, "Will this get me what I want?" (Just keeping it real here, ladies.)

Throughout my journey, I've found that I am very much like Peter in Matthew 26:31–35.

It's the Last Supper, and Jesus has just told the disciples that on that very night, they will all fall away from him.

As soon as Peter hears the words, he's shocked. Why, he would *never!* How could Jesus even think such a thing! Didn't Jesus understand that Peter loved him—that he was "all in"—that he would do ANYTHING for him? Wasn't Jesus aware of the sacrifices that Peter had already made?

Sincerely believing it to be true, Peter passionately replies, "Even if I have to die with you, I will never disown you."

The thing about Peter is that he truly meant it.

However, Jesus understood that some things in Peter's heart and mind had to truly die before Peter would ever be able to stand behind the words that were coming from his mouth.

Peter's heart had to be broken. Peter needed to see that some parts of his heart were still following Jesus for what *Peter* could get out of it.

Ultimately, in John 21, Peter needed to be confronted with the question, "Peter, do you love me?"

Do I love Jesus enough to give my whole life to his service even if it means I don't get what I want?

What if Jesus' plan for my life doesn't even remotely resemble the dreams or aspirations I had for myself? Do I love him enough to still follow?

You see, Peter couldn't keep his commitment to give up everything for Jesus until he first realized one thing: To follow Jesus, all of Peter's plans had to die.

John 21:17–20 says,

The third time he said to him, "Simon son of John, do you love me?"

Peter was hurt because Jesus asked him the third time, "Do you love me?" He said, "Lord, you know all things; you know that I love you."

Jesus said, "Feed my sheep. Very truly I tell you, when you were younger you dressed yourself and went where you wanted; but when you are old you will stretch out your hands, and someone else will dress you and lead you where you do not want to go." Jesus said this to indicate the kind of death by which Peter would glorify God. Then he said to him, "Follow me!"

"All to Jesus I surrender, all to him I freely give."

The words are very popular; but living the sentiment is the greatest challenge you'll ever face in life.

It's easy to answer an altar call when you're seven and say, "I'll follow you wherever, whenever, however," but still keep a few caveats in your mind of what that really means. It's much harder to build a personal altar in your heart and say, "Seriously, WHATEVER you want—even if it means that I don't get what I really want—I love you enough to say WHATEVER."

That's when things really begin to change.

I don't have a story to go along with the day that I made a true WHATEVER commitment in my life. It didn't happen in response to an altar call or a dramatic sermon. I doubt it was even a moment in time.

It was more of a process—a daily surrendering.

It didn't come during an anointed, Pentecostal moment but, rather, through many moments of pain, heartache, and grief. It came choice by choice, decision by decision, hurtful comment by hurtful comment, through points of despair and hopelessness when it would have been easier to take the reins in my own life and say, "I'm taking control now and doing what I need to do to get what I want."

In those times when that option was so tempting, a quieter resolve was kept. Somewhere along the way my answer to the cries in my own heart and the criticisms of others became, "My life is not my own—I gave it away a long time ago. I will follow Jesus wherever he leads—even if I never get what I want."

All I ever wanted was to be married; yet, I am a happy, fulfilled, completely satisfied Christian single woman.

How can that be?

It doesn't make sense.

I didn't get what I wanted—only God knows if I ever will.

Why aren't I miserable, bitter, disgruntled, and empty?

Because somewhere along the journey I learned one of the keys to being happy and fulfilled in life, whether you're married or single: It isn't about me.

I was not created for the purpose of making myself happy by getting everything I wanted.

Each of us was created for the exclusive purpose of having a relationship with God and fulfilling the plan that he has for our lives.

Whether you're married or single, fulfilling that purpose is the ONLY way you will experience true joy, fulfillment, and satisfaction. It's the only road to finding your real value and worth. Even if all the dreams you have for your own life come true, if you don't have a personal relationship with Jesus and you aren't living out the plan he has for your life, you will never be happy.

We weren't meant to keep our lives, we were meant to find them by giving them away (Matthew 16:25).

Does this mean you'll never get what you want?

Quite honestly, I don't know what God has planned for you. However, if what you really want is joy, peace, contentment, and satisfaction, then what you really need is a change in perspective. You have to stop living for what you want and start seeking what God wants for you.

That's the key to living a life you will love.

It's the most crucial decision you'll ever make as a woman.

Will you go along with God's plan for your life, whatever it may be, or will you do what you need to do to get what you want?

It's an age-old struggle—starting with Eve in the garden of Eden.

She had everything; yet she chose to disobey God to fulfill her desire for the one thing she couldn't have. She didn't trust that everything God had given her was good, and that everything he kept from her was for her good.

Daily, we all live with the results of her choice.

So often we think, "Why did Eve make such a stupid decision?" Yet the same question could often be asked of us.

I don't know about you, but I don't want to follow in Eve's footsteps.

I want to trust God enough to lay my desires, designs, and questions aside and accept what he's given, knowing that he is a loving Father who gives what is best for his children when it is best for them.

I want to follow Peter's footsteps and commit to following wherever Jesus leads, even if it means going where I don't want to go, simply out of love for my Savior.

Daily I want to make the choice to give my life away so that I can find a life more abundant than I could ever imagine.

While I can say that for most of my life all I really wanted was to be married, at this point in my life I can honestly say that all I really want is Jesus.

Dear heavenly Father, you understand the struggle inside our hearts to desire things that may not be your will for us at this time. Many of these struggles are natural and normal, yet following your path for our particular lives may take us outside of the normal. Today, help us to fully surrender every area of our hearts to you. Help us to trust you enough to fully give you our lives and say, "Wherever you lead, I will follow." In Jesus' name, amen.

• the next step •

1. what is the most difficult thing for you to surrender to God?

2. have you ever made a commitment to God, yet had your own preconceived ideas about what that commitment meant?

3. how did you respond when God's ways were different than your own? after reading this chapter, do you think you need to change your response in any way?

4. do you love Jesus enough to surrender your whole life to his will even if it means you don't get what you want?

5. list the areas in your life that you are choosing to surrender.

chapter 2 • jennie

choosing obedience

Over two years ago, my husband of ten years walked out on my daughter and me. And in the blink of tear-filled eyes, my life was turned upside down and I became a single mom.

I'm sure many of you know the feeling of watching chaos unfold before you and the sudden weight of knowing you are the only one that can pull it all together. Quite honestly, it's overwhelming, and the temptation to just let yourself become completely run over and destroyed stands at the forefront of your mind as the easiest solution.

In that moment of swirling chaos, I stopped, looked up, and asked God, "What now?"

In those havoc-wreaking, heart-stabbing, room-spinning moments, I stood still and God met me. But I was faced with an immediate decision.

Do I do what comes most naturally and respond my way, by fighting chaos with chaos? Or do I wait until God instructs me how to move?

I am positive that I am not the only one who's been subjected to such a mess. And I sense deep in my heart that there are women reading this who have had a mess similar to mine dumped on them. You are just wanting to know when you'll feel like you can breathe again because the mess is suffocating you.

I also want to address those women directly that have been the cause of a mess. Your choices and actions may have caused others pain, chaos, and hurt.

Jesus is prepared to meet you in the middle of your mess today!

I had always strived as a Christian to "look like Jesus." This often gave me an unrealistic expectation that all of my messes should be packaged in neat and pretty little boxes that I was even somewhat proud to show off. It was easy to do when my messes were small enough to tidy up so efficiently. It wasn't until my mess resembled a dump truck full of waste and slop that had been emptied over me that I realized all I can do is cry out to God to help me clean up. I could almost hear an angel of heaven announce, "Clean up on Aisle 5!"

We get so focused on trying to display to others how much we look like Jesus, when we should really be relaying our constant need for him. How much more accessible Christ will seem to those around us when we are real about this.

I encourage you to just lay everything at the feet of Jesus and let go of all that is weighing so heavily upon you. Jesus has always made a point to seek out the messiest people and share a meal with them or sit with them beside a well.

He is ready and waiting to step in to help you as soon as you let him.

And as God directs you, begin to reach out to the women that God brings into your life who are hurting and broken. I am so grateful for the many women who weren't too uncomfortable to meet me and embrace me when life was its ugliest. They stood by me and have carried me in prayer. And many times, they have stepped in to meet very practical needs. Being like Jesus means embracing the mess.

Strive to be the woman who wakes up each day and says to God, "Okay, what do you have planned for me today?" Choose to hand the control of your life back over to the Lord and heed his direction for every moment.

Live a life of integrity by remaining obedient to the Holy Spirit, even when it is difficult.

All it takes is one obedient step after another. Just like a child learning consistent obedience to her parents, you won't always get it right. Sometimes you will even whine and complain about the task, but his steady hand will continue to guide you and instruct you in the way he wants you to go. When you choose to obey, your life reflects your sweet dedication to your heavenly Father. The more you listen to his voice and obey his instruction, the easier it will get. You will begin to reap the rewards of an obedient lifestyle rather than one with the constant pain of consequences and redirection.

If you want to choose this walk in righteousness but aren't sure where to start, open the Bible. Start filling your mind and heart with his truth and love for you. Once you know and can recognize truth, you will begin to see when other things in your life are not lining up with it. Allow those things that don't measure up to fall away.

Before you know it, you will be hearing the voice of God in your life and acting on it immediately, without hesitation. And suddenly you will be walking in the peace and grace and fullness that God desires for you to have in this life.

Don't beat yourself up and self destruct if you don't get it right every time. Embrace God's correction. Repent and turn back toward him, choosing to make better decisions next time. It's kind of like choosing a healthier lifestyle of eating: one "off-plan" meal doesn't mean that you throw out the whole healthy lifestyle and dive into a life of binge-eating every sugary substance that crosses your path. It's the same with your Christian walk.

Just because you sin and continue to slip up does not mean you throw everything away and give up, letting sin consume you. Just stop. Evaluate where you are and why you keep making poor decisions. You may need to make some drastic changes in your life.

Just like cleaning all the junk food out of your pantry before a diet, you may need to clean up areas in your life causing you to trip up and pull you further from God. This may mean that you have to stop hanging out at certain places, being with certain friends, watching certain shows or movies, reading certain books or magazines. Cleaning the areas of junk or temptation out of your life is not a form of legalism, it's WISDOM. An alcoholic is wise not to hang out in a bar or be with friends while they are drinking. For some, they cannot even eat a dessert or food that may have the taste of wine or liquor cooked into it, as the taste will trigger their old habits. It is the same with our Christian walk. If it is difficult for you to resist certain areas of temptation, don't allow them in your home. Don't go near them in social settings. You may need to be extreme in some areas until you are able to gain self-control.

Get a good accountability partner: a godly woman who is going to be the voice of reason when you are trying to justify why you are settling into old habits. Choose a woman who will pray with you when you are weak, and who will speak truth and life to you when the lies of the enemy are trying to sway you.

You are never too far gone or too messy for God to clean up and restore. Your life is never too broken or damaged for God to fix it. It's simply a matter of choice on your part. Minute by minute, day by day, choosing to act in obedience to his Word and his voice in your life.

You can choose to live a life of obedience now!

Dear heavenly Father, Thank you for choosing me even when I haven't always been faithful to choose you. Help me to seek you and find you in the middle of my messy life. Help me to recognize and remove anything in my life that is taking your place in the center of my heart. I invite you into my life to be my guide and direct my steps. Please bring godly women into my life that will challenge and encourage me to

walk in your ways and speak your truth. I commit my life to you this day. In Jesus' name, amen.

• the next step •

1. what "messy" areas in your life are in need of cleaning?

2. what are some ways you've been able to be obedient? disobedient?

3. name some women that you can either embrace in their mess, or ask to be with you to navigate through yours.

4. what do you need to remove or change to walk forward in obedience?

chapter 3 • jennie

choosing the right relationship

*B*ased on the title, one might assume this chapter is filled with helpful tips on how to find the perfect guy so that you can have the perfect relationship you've always dreamed of. This is mostly true, except the "perfect guy" has always been right there waiting for you. At the risk of sounding cliché and Christianeesy, I'm implying that you should shift your focus from finding your husband to seeking out and spending time with your heavenly Father.

I used to dread going to church prayer meetings. How's that for utter honesty?

I would always go, of course. Because that's what any good pastor's kid or pastor's wife was expected to do. Right? (Insert massive eye roll here.)

I would typically get through my little list of requests for the Lord in about ten minutes. And that was being as wordy as possible. Then, I would start to daydream or, in the days of early motherhood, sneak in a quick nap and call it "resting before the Lord."

Don't get me wrong; I've always loved the Lord and would enjoy these times in his presence. Amazingly, I would often leave having heard something specific from him and even feel refreshed in my spirit. This will happen any time we quiet ourselves before God and give him room to speak. But I always felt this awkwardness trying to converse with God initially. This was always hard for me to figure out.

I loved the Lord.

I read my Bible regularly.

I was surrendered to his will.

So why was it so difficult to get dialogue going when specific time for prayer was set aside?

Think about a time when you met up with an old friend for coffee or you were starting a conversation with someone you just met.

Remember how intentional you were trying to be in choosing topics to discuss or things you were willing to share?

Certainly, you hadn't opened up your whole heart to either type of person (or at least, not in a while). Because of lack of regular communication or start of a new relationship, you were limited in what could be discussed without filling in details from the past.

Now think about your conversations with your best friend or someone who knows you better than anyone. Sometimes all you have to say is one word or even make one facial expression or glance of the eyes and you have communicated enough to have you both rolling with laughter.

This connection only happens when you've spent time with a person. You have to share experiences, good and bad, and walk through them together to be able to jump back into deep conversation with the person or share a meaningful glance. You don't keep secrets from one another. You are able to be completely open and honest about all that you are thinking and feeling and you can entrust these feelings to your friend.

It is exactly the same with our relationship with God. The more time we spend communicating with him, the more we invite him to be part of our day, and the less we try to keep from him, the deeper our relationship will grow.

Search for the Lord and for his strength; continually seek him (1 Chronicles 16:11 NLT).

Share your hurts, fears, desires, anger, pain, and grief with God. He wants to hear all of it. Let him be the first one you share that job promotion or sale on clothes with. He just wants that time with you. Every moment. The highs and lows.

Don't worry about anything; instead, pray about everything. Tell God what you need, and thank him for all he has done (Philippians 4:6 NLT).

In our relationships with friends, we can't just go to them only when we need something. A really good friendship isn't based on one person constantly asking for things and the other person always giving. That will get old pretty quickly! And the relationship can only grow so deep. Granted, there are times when we walk through difficult circumstances and we tend to be more needy. These are the times that we need to be intentional about sharing the good moments, though they may be fewer and farther between, with those around us. We also need to do whatever we can to bless others during these times.

Devote yourselves to prayer with an alert mind and a thankful heart (Colossians 4:2 NLT).

It is certainly necessary to take every need and request and fear and worry to the Lord, but also be mindful in everything to give thanks. No matter what troubles come, find *something*, no matter how small, to praise God for. Sometimes, when we are faced with a great need and we step back to take inventory of what we already have, suddenly the lack doesn't seem as great. It makes it easier to trust God to come through because we are reminded of what he's already done and is capable of.

Once I developed a steady dialogue with God throughout my day—sharing the good, the bad and the ugly (especially of my heart), I was able to set aside hours at a time to sit in his presence without napping or daydreaming. I could communicate with him and desired to spend time with him. I found it much easier to hear his voice for direction and to obey him when faced with obstacles.

Make the decision, today, to be more intentional about communicating with him. Getting ready for work, driving in the car, in the checkout line at the grocery store, the waiting room at the doctor's office…whenever, wherever, talk with your best friend, your heavenly Father.

Pray continually (1 Thessalonians 5:17).

• • ⬤ • •

Do you fail miserably at accomplishing the goals and plans you desire to achieve regarding your devotional time with God? Do you set your level of expectation a little too high? Are your goals unattainable for your everyday life and schedule? Are they practical?

I've certainly done this before when trying to establish a consistent devotional time. One year, I resolved to get up a few hours earlier each morning to set that time aside to pray and read my Bible. I was already exhausted all the time, and getting up for work entailed a daily power struggle to not hit the snooze button over and over. When it came time to read at five o'clock in the morning, I was nodding off in mid-sentence and didn't retain one bit of what I was reading. I'm sure God appreciated my heart, but my efforts weren't effective.

I'm not sure why, but it was stuck in my head that to be a "true" woman of God, I needed to be spending a minimum of one hour in prayer and devotion before the Lord at the very start of my day. Finding a solid uninterrupted hour in my day while working, raising a small child, and ministering in a local church seemed next to impossible. I felt as if I was constantly letting myself and God down by not meeting my own ridiculous expectations (this has been a running theme in my life).

Once I grasped that the Lord wasn't just looking for us to "clock in," I was able to give myself a break. I began to look for moments in my day when I could steal away to read my Bible, pray, or listen to his voice. It was more sporadic and unscheduled than my type-A personality cared for, but it was also much more effective than my previous frustrated efforts. I found that, collectively, I was spending more time reading and praying than ever before, and I was including God in my entire day.

As life and schedules have changed, I've learned that it's okay to adapt. It doesn't have to look the same every day for you to be "spiritual" or "godly." On those days when you need to be out the door before seven o'clock, don't beat yourself up for not getting up before the roosters! Maybe start your day listening to worship music as you get ready, or turn on your audio Bible for the commute.

One thing I love about technology is the convenience of having my Bible, devotions, and worship music with me at all times. I've downloaded an app on my phone that has my Bible and a wide variety of daily devotional plans that I can choose from and even check off when I've read for the day. I can be at my daughter's cheerleading practice, waiting at a doctor's office, eating lunch, or squeezing in a few minutes of reading before I drift off to sleep. Being intentional about stealing these moments has amazed me with the increased amount of Bible reading and devotional time I've been able to obtain cumulatively.

If you are struggling to see where in your day you would be able to add anything extra, start by asking God to reveal to you the "unnecessaries" in your life.

There was a season of my life where I was trying hard to add time with the Lord into my day and struggled to make it a daily discipline. After a week or so of being frustrated with myself for not getting out of bed before anyone, make my coffee, and sit alone to read, I had a major revelation. I realized that my daughter was acutely aware of when my feet hit the floor and that is when she would get out of bed and be ready to place her breakfast order. I also realized that the first thing I did, before stepping out of bed, was grab my phone next to my bed and check all my emails and most recent Facebook statuses. Sometimes, twenty to thirty minutes later, I rolled out of bed and started my day disappointed that it was not going to be nearly as exciting as that of my "friends."

It was definitely time to readjust!

I began disciplining myself to immediately check in with God at the start of my day and absorb his truth and direction for my life. My perspective about daily tasks began to change and I was suddenly grateful for the people in my life and the opportunities that were ahead of me. So what if I wasn't snorkeling in Cancun or on a tour of Rome! Those days of adventure would have their place in my life too, but today, I was equipping myself to see God's purpose in doing my best with what was right in front of me.

I'm now living through a time where my schedule is inconsistent. Some days are very full and busy and I travel for weeks at a time, while other weeks are laid back and my mornings are wide open. The mornings I do have free, I enjoy fixing my morning cup of coffee, sitting on my back deck with my Bible and heart open to share time with God. These are moments I look forward to and thoroughly enjoy. I know that allowing him to pour into my heart and mind in my down time will carry me through the crazier times, and it will be much easier to find him in the midst of them.

Spending time absorbing the truth of God's Word is an invaluable asset to you in growing closer to God and becoming a woman who walks in obedience. Whatever season of life you are in, busy or calm, I encourage you to be intentional about weaving the Word into your day.

Dear Lord, I thank you for always being there even if I haven't taken the time to acknowledge your presence. I am sorry for the ways I have failed to include you in my life. I invite you to be a consistent part of my life. I recognize my need to speak with you and hear from you each day. Please help me to discover times in my day that could easily be filled with you and eliminate activities that are unnecessary. I look forward to the time we will be spending together and to sharing this journey with you. In Jesus' name, amen.

• the next step •

1. describe the ideal amount of time you'd like to spend praying and reading your bible and what that would look like?

2. what needs to be added to or removed from your daily schedule to make this more attainable?

3. set realistic, attainable goals to implement how you are going to make these adjustments and get started today!

chapter 4 • adessa

choosing to forgive God

One of my greatest fears in starting off this book with chapters about choosing surrender and obedience is that it will seem we're promoting a daisies-and-gumdrops, name-it-and-claim-it, if-you-build-it-they-will-come approach to living a victorious life in Christ.

We're not.

I'm well aware of the fact that a positive attitude and a spunky spirit won't heal hearts that are broken, heal deep disappointments, or suddenly make us happy in unpleasant circumstances. (At least it never worked for me.)

Still, the reason we felt it necessary to talk about these two topics first is that choosing surrender and choosing obedience are the on-ramps to all of the other choices you and I need to make to become satisfied, victorious Christian single women. Even on days when we make the wrong decision and detour into depression, wanting our own way, feeling sorry for ourselves, or, God forbid, downright disobedience to God's will for our lives, we'll once again have to pass through these two on-ramps of choosing surrender and choosing obedience to get back on course.

As we talk about all the other choices that will put us on the road to finding peace and joy in our season of singleness, we'll be facing these two areas over and over again. This includes the next choice we're going to talk about: Choosing to forgive God.

One of the first choices you need to make on your journey to living a joyful, fulfilled, victorious life is openly and honestly dealing with God. It's time to honestly lay your cards on the table.

Your life didn't turn out the way you hoped or planned.

God is supposed to be in control of your life and whether you're allowing yourself to openly ask this question or not, there's a place in your heart that's saying, *How could God let this happen to me?*

No matter how many times you read an inspirational Scripture or you listen to a "Buck up, Baby, everything is going to be all right" praise and worship song, deep inside your heart YOU ARE ANGRY.

I can tell you from experience that until you deal with your anger toward God, you will not be able to make any of the other choices that will lead to a happy and fulfilled life.

Here's my story:

As I said before, I was very young when I made a genuine commitment to turn my life over to God and serve him in full-time ministry. I was also very young when I made the assumption that this commitment automatically included marriage. From that point on the plan for my life was: Bible college, marriage, ministry—in that order.

After high school, I worked for a year to help pay for college, and then headed off to the University of Valley Forge near Philadelphia, Pennsylvania.

Looking back now I have to roll my eyes at the young girl who stood in line for freshman registration, wondering, "I wonder which of these guys will be the one I marry?" (Seriously, I was a goal-oriented person, and love and marriage were the next thing on my to-do list.)

Four years later, when graduation day came and I was not married, or engaged, or even dating anyone, I was devastated. On a day that should have been a celebration of successful achievement, all I felt was overwhelming failure, heartbreak, and disappointment with God.

It was a mixture of sadness and anger rolled into a giant, jumbled ball of emotions. When everyone stood to sing the old hymn "Great is Thy Faithfulness," I had to fight back the tears that were trying to blast through as my heart seemed to scream, "This is faithfulness? All I feel is let down, disappointed, and hopeless."

I remember telling someone that I felt like there was a basket filled with puppies looking for a home. One by one, people came and chose a puppy, loved it, took it home, and made it their own. Only I was the last puppy left in the basket—the puppy that no one wanted. Not even God.

Some of you may be thinking, "What a drama queen! This is quite the overreaction to not getting married in college."

But you need to understand; it wasn't 2015, when women stayed single longer. The opportunities for an unmarried woman in ministry were not what they are today. I honestly felt abandoned by God. I couldn't believe that I had surrendered my life completely to him, wanted to dedicate my life to his service, and he didn't want me. (Or so my distorted thinking told me.)

Even beyond my twisted ideas about marriage and ministry, I was also carrying around a broken heart. Because even though I was not in a relationship when I graduated, I had fallen in love during my four years in Bible college. The details aren't important anymore; suffice it to say that I was left very hurt and again very angry. Angry that God let things happen the way they did. Angry with people who made bad choices, and mostly angry that my perfect plans had fallen apart. Rather than dealing with my feelings in a healthy way, I pushed them down and plowed full speed ahead, letting the pain and anger build in my heart. (Not a good idea.)

Finally, add to the equation the fact that I was going home after graduation. Again, not part of my lifelong plan.

No, I had always imagined myself getting married, moving away, having an extraordinarily successful ministry and then coming back home once in a while to visit. My visions were to come back home as the conquering hero. Instead, when the ceremony ended, I was packing my bags and returning home with no job and (more importantly in my small town) no husband. Again, this was back before this was a common occurrence—I was breaking fresh ground and I was ANGRY.

How could God let this happen?

What could he possibly be thinking?

I had a plan for my life. I had goals. I probably even took the time to write them down, and I'm sure I must have sent him a copy. Didn't he get the memo?

This was not the way things were supposed to turn out!

Let's get really vulnerable and admit that I was really thinking thoughts like:

This is not fair. I don't deserve this. I played by all the rules—I kept up my end of the bargain. Sure, I wasn't perfect but I never did anything REALLY wrong.

I even compared myself to other people who hadn't kept God's rules as faithfully as I did (please understand those last few words were written with a roll of the eyes at my youthful self-righteous attitude) and asked God, "Why are their lives working out when they did this, this, and this? I didn't do any of those things and I get the short end of the stick!"

I was so angry and so hurt (the two emotions are usually pretty intertwined for me). Every ounce of emotion was being pointed directly at God, saying, "This is YOUR fault!"

This went on for several weeks. Looking back, I feel so sorry for my family who had to live with me!

I refused to unpack and accept the circumstances.

I tried everything I could to get out of the situation.

God didn't move (which just made me angrier).

Finally, my mom strongly encouraged me to go to counseling with a pastor who didn't feel sorry for me, didn't pity me, and didn't even help me get out of my circumstances. Instead, he told me to start reading a book that dealt with the battleground of the mind using the story of Peter—a man who followed Jesus only to be faced with intense disappointment when Jesus' plans didn't turn out to be the grandiose takeover of Rome that Peter imagined.

Trust me, I could relate. Like Peter, I had preconceived ideas of what "following Jesus wholeheartedly" meant. I understood the battle that was raging inside of Peter, who on the one hand really did want to love God and serve him wholeheartedly, yet on the other hand, was disappointed when God's plans were so different from his own.

What was the answer for Peter?

A heart-to-heart, no-holds-barred, time-to-get-real conversation with Jesus. A walk along the beach where Peter could face his own failure, choose once again to submit to God's plan whatever it may be, and get back to the business of following Jesus.

Like I said, I could relate.

I had two choices: I could allow my anger and disappointment to continue controlling my life, abandon my commitment to follow God's plan for my life, take the reins and start pursuing my own dreams, or I could get real with God, face my anger, pain, and disappointment, reconcile our relationship, and get back to the business of following Jesus via the on-ramp of surrender.

Heart to heart, sister to sister, from a heart of love I need to tell you that each of us needs to come to the place where we choose between these two options.

Are you going to deal with your anger or let it control you? Will you even admit it's there or keep denying it and running away from it?

Are you ready to get real with God or will you keep walking away from him?

I know it seems like there should be a third option. It sounds harsh to say that you can't continue to harbor anger and resentment toward God in your heart and follow him. But it's true.

You see, God wants to have an intimate and personal relationship with you. When you don't deal with your anger and pain, it becomes a barrier in that relationship, causing you and God to grow further and further apart. Even though you may still call yourself a Christian, be involved in church, and do all the right things, until you actually take down the wall of anger and pain, it will always stand in the way of developing a healthy relationship with God.

It's like the married couple who still live in the same house, still file joint tax returns and show up together at parties, but inside the house they don't talk, they live separate lives, and even sleep in separate rooms. It looks like they are married, but they don't really have a marriage relationship. He lives his life and she lives hers. It's a charade.

There are lots of Christians who are living the same charade with God. Technically, they are going through all the motions of being a Christian, but at some point they let anger, heartache, or disappointments destroy their relationship with him. Rather than facing the fact that they have issues with God, they choose to let those issues become a giant wall. Because of unresolved issues, they live their lives the way they want to and check in with God when it's appropriate. Some walk away from God altogether, but many more simply fall into the pattern of a loveless, fruitless version of Christianity.

They have a relationship with their pain and anger, but not with God.

Sadly, I've known too many people who made this choice. When faced with genuine disappointment, heartache, or tragedy, they did not choose to get real with God. Though they didn't use words, their actions said, "God let too many bad things happen to me, he let me suffer too much pain—I'm done trusting him. I'll handle things from now on. I'll keep going to church and saying I'm a Christian—but I'm in control now." Either consciously or unconsciously, they made the choice to let unforgiveness toward God rule their lives.

My prayer for you as you're reading this chapter is that you will not repeat their tragic decision. No matter what circumstances caused the anger and pain in your life today, whether it be the death of someone you loved, a divorce, a life-altering disappointment, an unexpected disease, or any other painful situation, I hope this chapter will help you to choose a different road. Rather than allowing your feelings and pain to destroy your relationship with God, make the choice to do whatever is necessary to restore your relationship with him.

Understand that it's okay to be honest with him. He is not shocked at all by the way you feel. There is nothing you could tell him that would surprise him, offend him, or make him stop loving you.

He already knows what's going on inside of you. He sees every tear you cry and he hears every angry thought and accusation that passes through your mind. He is already aware that you're angry with him. In his compassion he sees beyond the anger into the confusion and pain and fear at the heart of it all.

He's not waiting to judge you or condemn you for these emotions. Instead, he's calling to you, saying, "Come, let us reason together. Let's deal with this—let's talk it out. Together we'll get it all out in the open, deal with the pain in your heart, begin the healing process, and move forward together."

That's our heavenly Father's heart.

Healing. Restoration. Renewed fellowship. This is what he desires.

It all begins when you make the choice to get real with God.

At this point, some of you may be asking, "But how do I begin?" Perhaps the idea of being completely open and honest with God is a new concept for you and you're wondering, "Is it really okay to be totally vulnerable with God? After all, he is God."

Let me assure you that I've learned from personal experience that the best place to start is with total, complete, and open honesty. Get alone with God and tell him exactly how you feel.

Please trust me when I say that it's nothing he hasn't already heard before.

If you don't believe me, take a quick perusal through the Psalms and the Prophetic Books. These books of the Bible are filled with godly people who had deep personal relationships with God, pouring out their hearts and sharing the good, the bad, and the "oh-my-goodness-I-can't-believe-they-just-said-that."

One of my favorite examples is the Old Testament prophet Jeremiah. (The books of Jeremiah and Job also happen to be my two favorite books in the Bible, so read into that what you want.)

Jeremiah was God's man—his mouthpiece to the nation of Israel at this time. Jeremiah was also a really emotional guy. When he had a feeling, he REALLY felt it.

Throughout the book of Jeremiah, it's obvious that the prophet had some very strong feelings about some of the things God was allowing in his life at the time. Here's a few select passages that will show you what I mean:

Jeremiah 20:7–10 (The Message)
You pushed me into this, GOD, and I let you do it.
You were too much for me.
And now I'm a public joke.
They all poke fun at me.
Every time I open my mouth
I'm shouting, "Murder!" or "Rape!"
And all I get for my GOD-warnings
are insults and contempt.

Jeremiah 15:15–18 (The Message)
You know where I am, GOD! Remember
what I'm doing here!
Take my side against my detractors,
Don't stand back while they ruin me.
Just look at the abuse I'm taking!
When your words showed up, I ate them—
swallowed them whole. What a feast!
What delight I took in being yours,
O GOD, GOD-of-the-Angel-Armies!
I never joined the party crowd
in their laughter and their fun.
Led by you, I went off by myself.
You'd filled me with indignation.
Their sin had me seething.
But why, why this chronic pain, this ever worsening
wound and no healing in sight?
You're nothing, GOD, but a mirage,
a lovely oasis in the distance—and then nothing!

And you think God is going to be shocked or offended by what's on your heart! Go through the Bible and see that it is completely normal (even healthy) for God's people to speak to God openly and honestly about their pain, disappointments, and anger toward him. You can see it in the life of Job, David, Moses, Habakkuk, and many other godly men and women who made the choice to get real with God rather than let their anger take root and ruin their relationship with him.

There is nothing wrong with pouring out your heart to God as long as you don't stop there. This is just step one on the road to healing and restoration. As with any relationship, it's perfectly normal for there to be times when the two parties in a relationship sit down and say, "We've got to talk about some problems and truthfully lay all of the issues on the table."

There's an old saying that says, "Nothing clears the air like a good fight."

However, after the air is cleared, reconciliation comes when the two opposing sides come together to start picking up the pieces.

It's the same way in your relationship with God: After you've poured out your heart and emptied out your anger, you need to keep moving forward in the process and begin to reconcile your relationship with him.

The next step in reconciliation is your choice to forgive God.

I know it sounds ridiculous and, again, maybe even a little like heresy. After all, did God do something wrong that we need to forgive him?

No, God never does anything wrong. He never sins and he never makes a mistake.

Our choice to forgive God has nothing to do with him; it's about us. We need to make the conscious choice to stop blaming God for the things he allowed in our lives.

It's coming to the place of resolving that even though you don't understand why God allowed what he did and you may not even like what he did, you're not going to allow your pain to build a wall of anger, confusion, and disappointment in your relationship with him. It's basically coming to a place of acceptance where you say, "I don't understand, but I'm going to trust you anyway and put my anger aside."

Of course, the next step in reconciling your relationship with God is asking him to forgive you for being angry with him and blaming him.

What?! Didn't you just say it was normal and even healthy to express your anger to God?

Absolutely.

Then why do I have to ask God to forgive me for feeling this way?

Well, just because you honestly feel something doesn't mean that your feelings were right. Being open and honest before God allows us to purge all of the anger, disappointment, feelings of betrayal, and pain from our hearts. Purging is the healthy part.

We ask God to forgive us because even though these feelings may be natural and normal, it is still a sin for us to be angry with God. True restoration of fellowship only comes when we not only admit that the sin is there, but we ask God to forgive it and take it away. That's when the healing process can really begin.

You see, it's not a sin to feel anger toward God in the heat of the moment; however, it is a sin to allow unconfessed anger to take up residence in your heart. When we confess our sin of anger, we're giving it an eviction notice that says, "You're not welcome here anymore…I'm choosing my relationship with God over my feelings."

As we talked about at the beginning of the chapter, it's the choice to forgive God and stop blaming him for our lives and to ask his forgiveness for being angry and disappointed in him that puts us back on the on-ramp of surrendering our will to God's will and choosing to live contentedly in the circumstances he's allowed.

It's those three steps—honesty, forgiveness, and surrender—that help you get off the destructive road of anger and take those first few steps toward living as a victorious Christian woman.

I know from experience that these choices are not always easy. I'll even warn you that at times those old voices of anger and "God doesn't really love you or he wouldn't allow these things to happen to you" may try to reappear. I know that in my own life there were years where the struggle between what I wanted and God wanted would try to reemerge, attempting to build a wall in my relationship with God. Yet, every time, it was my CHOICE to get real with God and say, "This is how I feel, but I'm setting my feelings aside for the sake of our relationship," that helped me stay on God's path for my life and ultimately find satisfaction, peace, and joy.

After years of fighting the battle between what I want and what God wants, I've learned that even when I can't see it, even when it makes no sense to me, and even when it's painful, God always has a plan to use everything he allows in my life for his good and the good of his kingdom. God doesn't waste anything.

Just like he did in the life of Joseph, a young man who was sold into slavery and then falsely imprisoned because of other people's sinful choices, God makes something good out of every disappointment that has happened in your life. Only your choice to let unresolved anger, resentment, or disappointments lead you on a path of rebellion away from his plan for your life can stop God from making a treasure from your tragedy.

Don't make that choice. Instead, every time you want to blame God or be angry with him, make the choice to get real with him.

Be open, be honest, be real, and then be repentant.

Always make the decision to trade your heartache for his healing by bringing your pain to him and re-surrendering your will to his ways. Choose to get real with God and choose to forgive him; then see if you don't ultimately discover that God has a plan and a purpose for every detail in your life.

• • • ⬤ • • •

Dear heavenly Father, I come to you in Jesus' name, admitting that it's time that I got real with you. I've been carrying this heartache and anger with me for far too long and it's been creating a barrier that's deeply hurting our relationship. Please give me the strength to come to you, to be honest with you, to truly open up my heart to you, and ultimately to lay my anger aside and completely surrender to your will for my life. Help me to trust that like with Joseph, you will take what was meant for evil in my life and use it for your glory. Amen.

• the next step •

1. have you ever been disappointed or angry with God?

2. what caused the anger?

3. how can anger with God interfere with your personal relationship with God?

4. how do you feel about the idea of having a no-holds-barred, open and honest conversation with God about your anger?

5. if it's normal for us to be angry with God, why do we need to ask his forgiveness?

6. what are you going to choose to forgive God of, and how will this benefit you?

chapter 5 • jennie

choosing to let go: take out the trash

I grew up singing the beautiful song, "I Surrender All." You know, the one that goes, "All to Jesus I surrender, all to him I freely give."

I never really took into account what that meant. Surrendering all seems so nice. The idealistic approach to Christianity of "Letting Go and Letting God."

"No more worries. No more stress. Be blessed and nothing less!"

That's a lovely idea. And there is an element of truth there when you finally arrive at the place of peace and rest in Christ, but often getting there is PAINFUL!

As we attempt to make changes in our lives, we try to establish new and better ways of doing things…get organized, eat better foods, exercise, stick to a budget. These are all great things to add to our lives and are certainly important for living well balanced. But in order for anything new to have a place to stay, we must remove what was there previously that was tripping us up.

Out with the OLD, in with the NEW!

I learned this as I was trying to find space in my daughter's bedroom for all the new toys and gifts she had received for Christmas. We were forced to go through her old toys and sort through what she still played with and get rid of anything broken, unwanted, or missing parts.

For my daughter, this is an especially difficult process. She is very sentimental and has experienced tremendous amounts of loss in the past few years. This makes it challenging to let go of anything with a memory or that may have a "potential use." We had to take our time with each item and weigh out its value for life right now.

Was it something she would still desire to have or still play with when the new stuff came in?

As we went further into the process, it became easier and easier for her to give away or toss anything she would no longer play with or had simply turned into junk over the years. Her focus shifted from trying to hold onto what was, to making room for NEW.

We may want an abundance of peace and joy and prosperity and love, but we have to make room for it. These things can't take their place if worry, fear, anger, and unforgiveness have settled in. This surrender, or letting go, of all the unnecessaries can be quite difficult and painful. Sometimes it requires you to be willing to go back to that hurt, the initial cause of the pain, look at it and process it and then lay it before the Lord. Hand it over to him. Our little hearts were not meant to carry the weight of such grief and pain. He is ready and willing to take it from us if we are willing to let go.

Whether you are trading bad habits for healthy ones or exchanging sorrow for joy, surrender it all to God and allow him to help you with the clean up.

For some, the process of letting go of the past is quite emotional and requires time to grieve and properly lay things at the feet of Jesus. They may even have to dig through their past and properly clean out messes they forgot about that are still taking up space. Others may be holding on to something that is in plain view, but they fail to see that it's getting in the way of them living the freest and fullest life. There's no difficulty in the letting go; the challenge rests in them becoming aware of its presence.

My parents just moved into a beautiful house near the beach in southern Delaware. I went to help them get settled in and unpack. Each day, my mom and I tried to make a point to take a break from unpacking and head to the beach. We had a lot of fun walking along the beaches and exploring quaint little shops.

One particular day, we headed to a boardwalk that contained all kinds of neat little eateries we were itching to try out. Being a bit of a "foodie," this kind of thing excites me like none other and my mom sure had no complaints as we tried various ice cream and coffee places each day. While in the boardwalk community, we spotted an Italian bakery/ice cream shop. All I can say is, this had "JENNIE" written all over it!

We each ordered one of Nonna's featured flavors and sat in the little shop to enjoy our treat. We even got to enjoy conversation with Nonna herself and learned some neat information about her family and the area. My mom and I were truly enjoying this escape from boxes and all the conversation and adventures we were having.

We then decided that since we filled up on coffee and local treats, we should walk it off on the beach. We headed out of the shop and crossed the street to the beach access. We were engaged in a conversation and our eyes were darting from one shop to the next trying to take in all that this amazing little area had to offer.

As we got to the other side of the street and were preparing to go out to the beach, my mom looked down at her hands and realized that she was still carrying both her empty coffee and ice cream cups. They had been empty since before we left Nonna's and she got so wrapped up in all that we were doing next that she forgot to toss them on our way out the door. Neither of us had noticed she was carrying the trash until it was in the way as she was trying to gather her things from the car to take on the beach.

We knew that she needed to throw it away before we headed out to the beach because it would hinder her from walking freely and enjoying the sights. It also would have made it more difficult for her to pull out her camera to capture a picture of the beautiful shore. She wouldn't have been able to fully enjoy the walk if she was focused on trying to not drop her little pile of trash. Our immediate steps after realizing she was carrying this was toward the nearest trash can.

I realized how easily we do this with things in our life that are just unnecessary. They may have served a purpose at one time, but now it may be time to let them go and throw them away as they may be getting in the way of you fully enjoying the new adventures you are on.

Anger, hurt, fear, and pain are all things that we will experience from time to time. They are natural responses to situations in our life. But as things calm down and God is wanting to move you out from under the weight of a situation and into a place where you can truly enjoy all that is around you, you have to let go of the things you've been carrying around.

God doesn't want you carrying unnecessary weight or trash. He wants you to experience all the freedom and joy and newness that life has to offer. As you draw closer to him, he will begin to expose those areas in your life that are no longer yours to hold on to. He will make you aware of the unnecessary and make it obvious that it's time to drop it and leave it behind. Run to the nearest trash can!

This is sometimes an uncomfortable process. It is often a little embarrassing to have these things revealed to us. We may feel foolish for carrying them around for so long without realizing it. We may wonder how we didn't notice it before or why it didn't seem to be an issue before. But all of a sudden, there it is in front of you: all kinds of ugliness from the past.

This is where grace steps in and mercy overflows. Now that you recognize it, you are responsible for it. You get to choose what to do with the extra things you are carrying. Some choose to hang on to them simply because they don't know any different and there is fear in the unknown. For some, the familiar (even if it's ugly) feels safe and secure. On the other hand, embracing the correction, heeding God's wisdom and choosing to live and act as he would have you will give you freedom to embrace all the new and amazing gifts he has for you. You won't be carrying or experiencing those pains from the past and you won't bear the consequences of them leaking out onto others, people you love and admire. His grace will be there for you as you embrace this process of growth and healing.

Take a moment before the Lord to acknowledge the trash you've been walking around with. As God reveals it to you, don't ignore it or hope it will go away on its own. Take action and allow God to do an amazing "clean up" in your heart and renew your mind. He loves you enough to correct you. He does this so you can change. You can be better and you can live in freedom and truth.

In order to receive all the NEW that God has for us, we need to be willing to lay down and clean out anything that is just taking up space in our lives and in our hearts. It takes an act of surrender before the Lord to allow him to chisel away all the things that we may feel are necessary to be there. He may be the only one who can see the NEW that's coming and he knows where you'll need room for it.

*For I am about to do something new.
See, I have already begun! Do you not see it?
I will make a pathway through the wilderness.
I will create rivers in the dry wasteland.*
Isaiah 43:19 (NLT)

• • • ⬤ • • •

Dear heavenly Father, today I surrender myself to you, including my past, present, and future. Help me recognize the old things that I've been storing or holding onto that no longer have a place in my life. Help me embrace the difficult process of letting go of these things. I desire to keep my focus on what good is ahead of me and I choose to let go of the painful things from my past. Thank you for the opportunity to live a free life. Lord, you are good. In Jesus' name, amen.

• the next step •

1. what are some things you are still struggling to let go of? be honest with yourself.

2. what NEW things would you rather be embracing or areas you'd like to see healed?

3. what do you plan to do that will help you make room for NEW?

chapter 6 • adessa

choosing to overcome your past

One of my favorite movie scenes comes from the Tom Hanks film *Castaway*. For those of you who've never seen the movie, Hanks plays Chuck Noland, a FedEx employee stranded on a deserted island after a plane crash that killed everyone else on board. After surviving at least four years on the island, Chuck manages to build a raft that takes him onto the sea where he is rescued by a passing ship.

Then comes my favorite part of the movie: When he returns to civilization, Chuck is faced with a new reality, starting with the fact that everyone had given him up for dead years ago. They had a funeral and legally he was dead.

Not only had his friends assumed he was dead, but his fiancé had moved on. She was now married with a young daughter. In the four-plus years that he was gone, everything had changed.

Out of all the dramatic footage in this movie, the last scene left the biggest impression in my mind. After facing all the changes and realizing that his old life was over, Chuck is faced with the question, *What now?*

After he delivers the one package that he didn't open on the island, he drives his truck to an intersection. Getting out, he stands in the middle of the intersection, looking north, south, east, and west. The movie ends with the unspoken question, *Where do we go from here?*

He'd survived the worst, now what?

I found myself asking this same question after I came home from college, re-surrendered my life to God's plan, and finally unpacked my bags. After I worked through my initial anger with God and chose to walk with him through this journey rather than blame him that life didn't turn out the way I wanted, I was faced with the question, *Now what?*

The floor had fallen out of my plans, the roof caved in, and I'd survived the worst thing I could possibly imagine at the time (which is funny because little did I know there were so many more difficult challenges to come). Still, I'd survived. Now where did I go from here?

Well, being a driven, type-A personality, I immediately started doing everything I could to start knocking down a door—any door—to get me back on a life path that made sense. Knowing that this wasn't what I truly needed most at the time, God did not allow any doors to open.

Instead, he had a different path. He knew that the first priority was making some major repairs inside of me. After banging my head against a few too many brick walls, I finally caught on to the road that God wanted me to take and settled in for a time of repairs.

One of the things I focused on during this time was my own personal relationship with Jesus. Honestly, the concept of having an intimate, open, honest relationship with God wasn't new to me. From a very early age, my mom guided us toward choosing a relationship with God over religion. Throughout my life, my prayer time was always very personal and vulnerable and I knew that God was my closest confidant. Not only was I very free in my conversation with him, but I knew how to listen and hear his voice guiding, directing, correcting, and speaking back to me. So it wasn't like this was something new.

However, during this time in my life, my relationship with God did go to another level. One reason was that I was committed to spending a significant amount of time with him in prayer and not just Bible reading, but Bible study. I was desperate—not just for him to make changes in my life, but for him to make changes inside of me. Out of my desperation came a hunger that only God could fill through times of dedicated prayer and Bible study as I chose to focus on deepening my personal relationship with him.

Not only was I filling my free time with more of God and his Word, but during this time I was also eliminating some things from my life. Specifically, I stopped listening to all secular music, and dramatically edited the quality of my TV and movie choices. I also gave up all fiction material, stopped reading all non-Christian woman's magazines or any other written material that was influencing my thought process.

In a way, I was going through a spiritual cleansing—purging my heart and mind of every influence that wasn't benefiting me. Let me tell you, it wasn't easy.

I've always been a big fan of romantic music and dramatic stories. Even though I knew better, when I went to college I indulged myself in romantic secular music, "chick flicks," and television shows that I should not have been watching. I was like a person who gorged herself on unhealthy food and then wondered why she felt sick afterward.

After four years of entertainment choices that did nothing but feed my already twisted thinking about love, sensuality, and relationships, it was time to end their influence. I went cold turkey and began starving some avenues that were creating appetites in my life that were contrary to God's plan and God's will.

This choice to turn off any negative or unnecessary influences in my life and focus on building my relationship with God allowed me to make another choice that radically changed my life: The choice to face and overcome my past.

You see, God knew (and I didn't realize) that issues from my past and my family's past were keeping me from being the woman that he created me to be. These issues were influencing my identity, my sense of self-worth, and quite frankly, they were twisting my thinking about life, relationships, and even God himself. Even though the next thing on my to-do list was finding a job or a husband so my life would make sense again, the next thing on God's to-do list was dealing with my past so I could find my identity as his daughter. The choice he led me to next was, *Are you willing to take a time out and overcome your past?*

I remember it like it was yesterday. We were driving home from church on a Sunday afternoon when the Holy Spirit starting revealing truth to me. The specific truth had to do with my relationship with my dad. For the first time in my life I was being forced to face the truth that it wasn't good and it was having a profound impact on my life.

To be honest, I wasn't really shocked that my dad and I didn't get along. Everyone knew that. My mom and my brother always joked that we got along like a cat and a dog—always at odds.

The truth that the Holy Spirit was forcing me to see on this Sunday afternoon was that it wasn't my fault. Believe it or not, that was a hard truth to face.

You see, even though it was obvious that my dad and I didn't agree on anything, I'd always seen it as my fault. (Mostly because my dad told me it was my fault.) I was rebellious. I was too driven. I wanted too much out of life. I was never satisfied. I was difficult.

My dad, on the other hand, wanted everyone to believe that he was basically perfect. He presented the image that he'd grown up in the perfect family where everyone got along and never fought. He understood life, relationships, and the world better than anyone else. He was the perfect Christian husband, father, and churchgoer. If anyone had problems, they weren't his; he was the victim. (Just a side hint I've learned over the years: whenever anyone has to be that "perfect," suspect hidden problems lingering just beneath the surface. No one or nothing in life is perfect.)

Still, this was the pattern in our family. Whenever there were problems in the marriage (even a minor fight or disagreement), my dad said my mom had problems that she needed to overcome. When my brother and I had issues, we were the problem. When my dad and I constantly butted heads because my type-A personality didn't fit into his definition of how a female should behave, I was unsubmissive, rebellious, disrespectful, or unappreciative of how great he really was.

This pattern started when I was about seven years old. I had just transferred from public school to Christian school and I loved it! Right away, because of the different environment and the self-paced curriculum, I began showing a marked improvement academically. Not only were my grades very high, but I was moving through the work at an accelerated pace. Soon I was working at least two years ahead of my grade level and loving every minute of it.

My dad was not so thrilled. He felt threatened. When I did well, he felt insecure. He assumed I was cheating and accused me of figuring out the system and moving through the work without learning. (This wasn't private; he also discussed it with my teachers.)

That set the tone of our relationship going forward.

The next ten years were essentially a battle as I was being myself while my dad tried to squash my dreams, personality, and capabilities to fit into his definition of what a female should be. Of course, I was always wrong and he was always right.

Instead of being proud and encouraging me to keep up the good work, his insecurities arose. The more areas where I excelled, the more he became hypercritical of everything I did. It was as if he always had to point out that he was smarter by criticizing me.

When I became a teenager, he told me I wanted too much out of life. He told me my standards were too high. Instead of supporting my dreams, he wanted to keep me in reality.

When I went to college and became the class president, he hated it. I had stepped way over the line of what a woman should do. I couldn't do anything to please him. My personality was too strong. I talked too much and too loudly.

Eventually, my dad's attitude toward me left me with a lot of confused ideas.

Is this how God felt about women?

Did God really want women to squelch their personalities and capabilities to make men feel better?

Did all men feel the way my dad did?

By the time I graduated from college, these questions were tying me up in knots. To a point, I had lost myself, trying to be the kind of woman a man would want. I was a chameleon.

Based on my dad's lies that there must be something wrong with me and no man would ever want to marry someone with my personality, I tried to contort my personality or abilities into what I thought would make me more appealing. If I was interested in a man, I did everything I could to become the woman I thought he'd want. The whole time the original me was all locked up in a box, while I was trying to be someone I wasn't. I wasn't happy and God wasn't pleased.

It was time to face the truth.

I wish I could tell you that facing the truth was a once-and-done experience, but I can't. Instead, it was a rather long process of facing as much truth as I could handle, processing it, choosing to believe the truth instead of lies, forgiving, and learning new ways of thinking. Like an onion, many layers of pain and lies had to be uncovered. With each layer there was pain, truth, healing, and ultimately freedom from the lies that were controlling me. Of course, as each layer was uncovered and healed, I also gained more and more freedom to stop believing lies and start being myself.

Still, it took time. Over the next few years, the Holy Spirit revealed a lot of truth and uncovered a lot of secrets. We eventually learned that in his need to appear perfect, my dad had lied about almost everything in his life from the first day he met my mom. The truth was that he had a lot of issues in his own life that needed to be uncovered and addressed. Rather than dealing with them, he chose to use manipulation, lies, and abuse to control the people in his life.

That was his choice, but in the end, the people in his life (my mom, my brother, and I) suffered the consequences. When the truth came out, each of us needed to make our own choice to overcome our past or let it control us and influence our future. Many times this choice required action.

Each of us had to choose to spend hours alone with God, praying through the issues of our hearts, remembering things we didn't want to remember.

Then came the choice to forgive my dad whether he was repentant or not.

I had to choose to study the Bible to learn new behavioral patterns I could apply to my life.

As a family and individually, we spent a lot of time in counseling and working with a minister trained in spiritual deliverance. There were so many knots that needed to be untied from all the years of lying, deceit, and abuse.

We did a lot of talking, and, individually, we all did a lot of journaling.

The healing and overcoming wasn't magical by any means. It took a lot of work and honesty, constantly choosing over and over again that we would allow God to take us through this entire process of overcoming our past and setting us free.

Although there were many years when I felt like Tom Hanks' character, stuck on a desert island, just trying to survive, I have absolutely no regrets that I chose to allow God to take this time in my life and set me free from my past. Without a speck of doubt, it was one of the best choices I made in my life.

Why?

Because I couldn't become the woman God wanted me to be, (I couldn't even be myself), or do any of the things he wanted me to do until the lies and abuse that were scrambling my heart and mind were healed. Until I dealt with my past, I was broken. All I had to offer God or anyone else was my brokenness—a twisted, distorted version of the woman God had originally created.

When I chose to agree with God and to allow him take me through the process of overcoming my past, God was able to heal my brokenness and replace it with wholeness and the opportunity to finally find my identity in him. That's when things really started to change.

You see, as God healed my past, I was finally able to find something I didn't even know I was missing until that point: my identity.

When the truth came out that my dad had lots of unresolved issues from his own life that were affecting his ideas about women, I was finally able to stop twisting my personality into what he wanted it to be. When the Holy Spirit revealed that my dad's ideas about men and women, submission, and relationships were wrong, I was able to take a deep breath and realize that I was not the problem. God created me exactly the way he wanted me to be to accomplish his plan for my life. I could stop trying to squash, kill, hide, or distort my personality to fit my dad's crazy ideas, and just be myself.

I was like breathing fresh air for the first time.

Once the truth came out, I was finally allowed to start loving myself—just the way I was, flaws and all. I began realizing that the only person I needed to care about pleasing was God. He liked me just the way I was—after all, he created me that way.

Sure, there were parts of me that he wanted to refine and reshape into the image of his Son, but the key word was "refine."

He wanted to take what he created and make it better—higher quality. The things he removed or added to my life were always for my good, to make me the best version of the woman he designed me to be. He didn't want to destroy me or squash my potential, but he wanted to refine it to produce even more life and health and peace.

Peace. There was a new word for me. Yet, as I stopped seeing my heavenly Father through my earthly father's eyes, I was able to find peace.

I didn't have to work so hard for approval because God already approved of me. As I learned to rest in his approval, I found that not only was I okay with myself, but I actually liked myself. It was okay to be who I was created to me—a driven, capable, funny, smart, opinionated woman of God who wants to make a difference in the world.

Yes, even though the time spent on overcoming my past wasn't on my agenda, it was THE BEST thing that could have happened in the lives of my mom, my brother, and me. The reason I'm writing this chapter and sharing all these things isn't to make myself look good or my dad look bad. Rather, I'm hoping that sharing this part of my life will help you make the same choice that I made: To allow God to take you through the process of facing and overcoming your past.

I understand that the term *past* doesn't mean the same for everyone. While I had to deal with my dad's abuse, your past may involve pain or damage from your mom, your grandmother or another adult, male or female. Maybe there was someone in your life treated you badly or constantly demeaned you. Perhaps it was a teacher.

Years ago I knew a lady who dreamed of being a teacher. She loved kids and wanted to help them. However, the first obstacle she had to overcome was her own memory of a teacher telling her she was stupid. This teacher was so mean to her that my friend was afraid to go to college to make her dream come true. Although she did eventually overcome her fears, it was a real battle for her to overcome the voice of a mean, critical teacher from long ago.

Of course, the term *past* doesn't always have to involve your childhood. There are women who are carrying around the wounds and scars from old boyfriends or former husbands. It would be great if all romances ended in happily ever after, but they don't. We live in a world where there are men who haven't dealt with their own issues; rather, they take their pain and frustration out on the women in their lives.

Sometimes the result is physical abuse. Other times the abuse is verbal and emotional. Don't kid yourself, verbal and emotional abuse can be just as painful as physical abuse, because rather than attacking your body, the abuser is attacking your mind, your personality, your spirit. He is injuring the very essence of who you are. Even after the relationship is over, many women still struggle with wondering, *Was he right about me? Am I the problem? Was I as stupid as he said I was?* This is only a small illustration of the thoughts and questions that go through a woman's mind after she has been mistreated by someone she loves.

The good news is that we have a God who specializes in healing and deliverance. There is nothing he wants more than to heal the damage in your soul. One by one, he wants to heal your memories, heal the damage done to your heart, and help you overcome your past and become the woman he wants you to be.

However, he cannot begin this process until you give him permission.

Once again, you are faced with a choice.

Do you want to continue living in the pain of the past, or do you want to be free?

Are you willing to face the past and bury it once and for all so that it stops damaging your future?

Will you allow God the time necessary to take you through this process, believing that everything he does is for your good?

I have to admit that when I first started going through the healing process, I hoped God would hurry up. I even prayed that he get it over with quickly so I could get back to my life.

However, God wasn't so concerned about me getting back to my old life or even hurrying up to get to the things I wanted out of life. Instead, he wanted me to start living life abundantly—free from the bondage and burdens that were controlling me. Free to live a life of joy and peace fulfilling his purposes for my life.

As John 10:10 says, Jesus didn't come just to help us survive life; he came to give us abundant life.

The road to abundant life begins as we once again pass through the on-ramp of choosing to surrender and begin the journey of choosing to let God do whatever he needs to do to help us face and overcome our past, knowing that the ultimate destination will lead to health, wholeness, peace, joy, and finding our true identity in him.

Will you choose to allow God to help you face your past and overcome it?

• • • ⬤ • • •

Dear heavenly Father, Once again I come to you, ready to make another choice. You know even better than I the things from my past that are keeping me in bondage, preventing me from reaching my full potential as your daughter. You know that I've tried to find my identity in many different things…relationships, accomplishments, and the approval of other people. You also know the things in my past that have kept me from truly finding my identity in you.

But today, Lord, I want to make a different choice. Today, I am opening the door for you to begin searching through the archives of my past and do whatever is necessary to clean out anything that is damaging my soul or creating lies in my mind. I surrender my plans, my timetable, and my agenda to you—giving you the time necessary to take me through this process. I'm tired of my past controlling me and telling me who I am. I want to start the journey of healing and learning who YOU created me to be. In Jesus' name, amen.

• the next step •

1. are there things in your past keeping you in bondage—preventing you from becoming the woman you'd like to be?

2. has your identity been distorted by another person's words, behaviors or ideas of "how you should be"?

3. do you want to continue living in the pain of the past, or do you want to be free?

4. how do you feel about taking time out of your life to focus on overcoming your past?

5. what proactive steps do you need to take to help you overcome your past? do you need to spend time with God, visit a counselor, or learn new behavioral patterns?

chapter 7 • jennie

choosing to forgive

forgiveness.

When most people hear this word, something inside them aches or twinges. It resonates with something deep that has most likely been suppressed or stuffed.

All of us, at one point, have been rejected, discarded, abused, hurt, abandoned, or denied. Because of this, every one of us are in a place where we must choose to forgive. Some wounds go so far back and are so deep that you wonder how God can ever fully heal them. All I can say is that he can and will but only if you let him.

The pain of my broken family and marriage is no secret. My ex-husband made his sinful mess a very public display that I was forced to walk through and navigate without warning. He became a very different person in the process and didn't care whose lives he was destroying or how his choices were affecting others. If there's anything I understand, it's rejection and abandonment and hurt.

To this day, I can look back to the whirlwind months after he left and remember the ache, turmoil, and agony that I felt deep in my heart. I'm grateful that now it's only a distant memory.

The pain isn't as real and present as it once was. At the time, pain was cultivating an energy charged by anger. This anger, quite honestly, is the fuel that helped me move out of my home in Ohio and into my parents' house in Pennsylvania, assist with running a conference for three thousand women, and still manage the care of my daughter, all within a two-week span of the man's departure.

In some ways, the energy from this anger was helping me to survive. I was able to numbly plow through all that was necessary to transition out of my old life (all I knew) into an unknown new "normal." As much as I needed all the energy I could get, I also found that, on many levels, this form of energy was exhausting to maintain and I needed to let go.

I had begun to feel this nudging in my heart to allow God to take this pain and anger. It was too heavy and too much for my heart to hold onto.

I was walking around with my views tainted by my pain. I was hurting and because of it, I was constantly on guard to protect myself from any new trauma. I expected everyone I ever trusted and cared for to betray me in some way. My beliefs about people in general became jaded.

As a nurse, I tend to view things in medical analogies and God has an odd way of relating to me in this manner to speak truth and bring revelation and healing in my life. So bear with me as I walk you through my journey.

The way I began to see my situation was in terms of an initial trauma or injury to the skin. Brokenness, bleeding, and pain as a result of an incredible unforeseen blow. In an attempt to just manage the bleeding and pain, the reality of the desperate need for medical attention went unrecognized. It's easy to get caught up in the hows and whys the trauma occurred and fail to realize the need for true healing and some assistance with the stitching (or closing) of the gaping wound.

I was just trying to keep from bleeding all over my family and friends.

I tried covering my wound with smiles and productivity. I thought if it was covered, cleaned up, and no one else was affected by it, then maybe the wound was healing and would eventually be okay. Because time heals all wounds, right?

What I didn't realize was that, even though my wound began to scab and heal over on the surface, the tissue underneath was still wide open and raw. Because I hadn't allowed God access to the wound, he wasn't able to do the necessary stitching to close it so that it would heal properly. Now every time that wound was slightly touched or bumped or pressed upon, the same excruciating pain seized the innermost parts of my heart. It was as though I was feeling the initial blow all over again.

As time went on and new offenses continued to occur, the wound would easily reopen and the rawness and underlying pain was revealed. A wound can only remain open for so long or be reopened so many times before infection will set in and wreak havoc under the surface. This complicates the preexisting wound and adds a whole new layer to the problem and pain.

There's an adrenaline rush with any new injury that kicks in to assist with the survival of the immediate trauma. As that wears off, the reality of pain sinks in.

We are capable of feeding off this adrenaline for quite some time as we push through in survival mode. It's one thing to have the pain of the original wound and the anger and frustration that goes with it. It's another to plow through it, not address what caused it, and just move forward trying to prevent any damage that may occur in the future.

I became overprotective of my wound and was guarded so that I would never have to experience such angst ever again. I didn't realize that my damage control didn't fix or heal my problem. In trying to manage on my own, I actually made matters worse. I didn't notice the underlying infection of bitterness and unforgiveness until I thoroughly allowed God access to all areas of my heart.

I'm grateful that this process came quickly for me along my journey as I had turned toward God in the moment my trauma occurred.

I listened to his voice for direction and guidance and was willing to obey his every word. I leaned on him for strength and cried out to him for peace.

The floods of grace in these moments were astounding, and I was acutely aware of his steady presence. Because I stayed close, he was consistent to reveal all that needed to change. I also knew that I could never imagine feeling this horrible ever again, so I might as well surrender and allow him to chisel away *everything* in my heart that needed to go.

Years of painful experiences and layers of scar tissue needed to be cut away. If I was going to allow him to address this most painful infection that was overwhelming my soul, then I figured it best to just remain under the knife to do a complete work and healing in my heart. All offenses, all hurts, and broken pieces were laid before him to excise and, with a steady, gentle hand, remove for good.

I made a conscious decision to do all that was necessary to allow God to make me better because of my circumstances. I refused to become a victim of someone else's foolish choices and be defined by that person's mess.

Like any surgery, the pain of the immediate cutting to get below the surface and address the nagging problem is a new wave of pain unlike the one you have been experiencing prior. It's sharp and intense and direct.

The difference is that it's intentional. You are surrendered to it and you know it's coming. You also know that your brokenness is in the hands of a trusted surgeon and you are confident that the outcome and long-term healing is going to be much more beneficial to your daily living and health.

When I finally surrendered to this process and was willing to let God do this work in me, I had to set aside specific time for it to take place. I scheduled my surgery.

I even picked the location and atmosphere that would be most conducive. I chose a quiet spot where I would have a significant amount of uninterrupted alone time.

I put on some worship music. Specifically, a song titled "You Know Me" that spoke the truth about God knowing the most intricate and ugly parts of our heart even if we choose not to acknowledge them before him. In recognizing that, God also revealed to me that he saw the beauty that was under the surface and by removing the yuck, he could allow that beauty to be seen.

When you are willing to allow God to perform this most intense heart surgery, be prepared to "ugly cry." I have never been one to cry a whole lot. I'm great at stuffing and stuffing till I explode. I realized I never gave myself the permission or opportunity to properly grieve and process. I was long overdue for a good cry—about everything! This was my opportunity to let it all out while in the protective arms of God.

I cannot speak to anyone else's experience of forgiving. But, for me, it definitely became more painful initially as I waded through and released every offense over to God. I had to let go of any mental control I thought I had that could maintain hope of future revenge. (As if I could mentally cause others to suffer remorse for their actions.) It seems laughable to think of it this way, but this is the bondage of unforgiveness that the enemy wants to hold us to. It's the unrealistic idea that the pain we feel daily will somehow be projected onto the person that caused it if we just hold on tightly enough. And that somehow, in releasing our pain, we are letting the other person off the hook. This is a blatant lie! At some point, we have all fallen into this trap until we are shown that handing that pain back over to God and choosing to forgive simply gives us the keys to let ourselves out of the prison we were forced into by our trauma. By letting go of our need to right our wrongs, we are unlocking the barred doors and stepping into a freed life.

I remember the emotional pain felt so intense that my chest ached and I thought I might heave as I released my will to fight for justice. It was a deep and painful cutting away as I acknowledged and looked at every area of hurt and then allowed God to take it. Though I wasn't exempt from the pain of this experience, the Holy Spirit immediately met me with a comfort and a grace. Similar to an anesthesiologist, he was there to provide me with all the peace I needed to stay on the operating table.

When I came to a place where I was open and real enough before the Lord to know that I had allowed him all necessary access to my heart and there was nothing left to be removed, I expected to feel immediately free and whole and full of joy. Instead, I felt raw and empty. I was disappointed as I felt I had done exactly what I was supposed to and I knew that the weight I had been carrying was gone. So why didn't I feel better?

In removing all that was causing me pain and anger and weighing me down, I was left with an open and gaping hole. There was another process in my healing that needed to take place for God to fully heal me. I had to let him fill me with all that *he* wanted to be there. In my recovery, it was important for me to get proper nutrients and rest that would provide what I needed to heal in a healthy way. I played worship music constantly, even as I slept, so that my mind always remained tuned in to an atmosphere of praise. And I read my Bible as much possible, feeding on all the truth and life that I could.

After a few days of this, I didn't feel so empty and I certainly wasn't in pain any more. I was able to hear God's voice much clearer and saw the world around me with his perspective. I was beginning to experience joy in the little things around me again.

My situation never changed and it actually got significantly worse for a season. But *I* had changed. I was better. I was whole. And with each new trauma or pain, I was willing to bring it back to God for immediate repair of my heart. I can recall other things that occurred during this time that were intensely painful. But I can also remember just as clearly the steady hand of God's provision and moments that were full of joy. Had I become stuck in my unforgiveness, my view would've been too jaded and clouded to see them and experience them fully.

Whether we feel like it or not, God's Word commands us to forgive others if we want our heavenly Father to forgive us (Matthew 6:14–15). It is an act of choice or free will. It is also an act obedience that will be greatly rewarded with peace, freedom, and true healing from past wounds and hurts. Giving the Lord access to all areas of your heart will be an invaluable step in your walk with him and will reap positive results in all avenues of your life.

Dear Lord, I approach you today as my Great Physician and I trust you with the wounds in my heart. Though I am uncertain, and maybe somewhat fearful, of what I will experience as I choose to forgive those that have deeply hurt me, I know that you offer healing and peace for those that make this choice. I surrender my brokenness to you. I am willing to allow you to cut away all that has infected my life and is continuing to cause me pain and grief. I ask that you reveal to me all the wounds that may need your touch. I am grateful for your gentle and steady hand. You are good and I trust you with my heart. In your precious name, amen.

• the next step •

1. who do you need to forgive and for what? make a list. depending on how long you've been avoiding this, the list may be quite long!

2. what women can be praying with you and for you as you embrace your need to forgive?

3. what's your plan? pick your time and place to get before the Lord, open your heart up to him and allow him to operate!

chapter 8 • adessa

choosing to overcome shame

*I*n November 2012, A Wellrounded Woman Ministries (another women's ministry that I lead) was presented with an amazing opportunity to promote the ministry at a women's conference in a neighboring state. As soon as I opened the email, I was thrilled! I couldn't wait to pack up our materials, hit the road, and tell lots of women that we'd never met before about our resource. Anyone who had seen me so excited would have thought I'd won a million dollars. I was psyched!

Over the next few days this excitement continued to grow as we planned the trip and God miraculously had someone donate all of the funds to cover the cost. (You thought I was doing a happy dance before—you should have seen me when that check came!) I was counting the days until the event!

Then another email arrived that put a damper on the party.

Don't get me wrong. It was a nice email.

It was from a college friend who saw my name on the list when she was helping to prepare the convention. Even though the email said, "Looking forward to seeing you," my heart sank when it arrived.

Immediately, my mind started imagining the conversation.

We'd say, "Hi," hug, tell each other that we don't look like we've aged at all (which isn't really true—at least, I look older), and then she'd ask the question, "So are you married…have any kids?"

And then I'd shrink. Even if she didn't say a negative word or give me one pitiful look, I'd feel ashamed—like I'd done something wrong.

I didn't fit into the mold or meet the expectations of other people.

Even though I'd overcome a lot in my life, I was still struggling with the fact that for me, being single was a tremendous source of embarrassment and shame. In this instance, it almost kept me from going to the conference and walking through the door that God had opened for our ministry.

The funny thing is, the problem that was causing me so much stress really had nothing to do with my relationship status. (Even if God had provided a Hallmark movie-style miracle and caused me to meet and marry the man of my dreams before the conference, this would not have solved my problem.) You see my problem wasn't a demographic issue; it was an issue of shame that needed to be overcome and conquered in Jesus' name.

What is shame?

The Free Dictionary defines it as a painful emotion caused by a sense of guilt, embarrassment, unworthiness, or disgrace.

It can be a mix of regret, self-hate, and dishonor.

Looking at these definitions, it's easy to see that shame can be a devastating problem. Sadly, it's a problem that is rampant among women today—even women within the church. It's a tool that the enemy of our souls uses to devour strong Christian women whom God wants to use to create a revolution in the world around them.

It's time shame's reign of terror ends!

You see, shame isn't just a problem for single women. True, it was the area of my life where I felt I'd failed to meet expectations, but other women struggle with the issue of shame in different areas.

Some women feel shame because of their weight or their appearance.

Others experience shame because of their lack of education or job experience.

Many women experience shame because of their past or their family background.

The problem with shame is that it doesn't focus on any one demographic; it tries to attack *every* woman at *every* economic, social, and age level, pointing out either her insufficiencies, insecurities, or the mistakes she's made in the past. Its goal is to cause you to be so overcome by the things you aren't or the things you've done that you become a prisoner.

Shame wants to control you.

It wants to make you hide away and never become the strong, godly, competent woman God created you to be.

That's really why the enemy of our souls uses this weapon on so many Christian women. He's afraid of what they could become if they allowed Jesus to control their life rather than shame. He's afraid of the life they'd live, the people they'd influence, and the difference they could make among their family, their friends, their community, and ultimately for the kingdom of God.

The best way the enemy knows to stop us is to attack us with shame. If he can make us feel unworthy, unloved, unwanted, and unnecessary, then there's always the chance that we'll agree with him and say, "You know what, that's right, I can't do what God wants me to do. I can't live the way God wants me to live and be the woman God's called me to be. Why am I even trying?"

It's one of the enemy's top strategies against women. However, thanks to Jesus, we can recognize this strategy and overcome it, throwing off the chains of shame once and for all and walking in the freedom of Jesus Christ.

How do we overcome shame? We need to develop some defensive war plans of our own. Let's look at some strategies together.

• we need to recognize shame for what it is: an attack of the enemy who wants to destroy us •

The first step in winning any battle is recognizing that you are at war.

When you are constantly being barraged with bombshells from an enemy, you are under attack. When you decide to fight back—you are at war.

For too long, Christian women have allowed the enemy to constantly attack them with the lies of shame, telling them they aren't good enough, they can never accomplish anything, they aren't worthy of God's love, and they have no potential. Because they are unwilling to fight the battle spiritually, lives are being destroyed and devastated by the enemy's terrorism.

However, this does not have to continue.

As God's daughters we can recognize that we are in a spiritual battle and choose to use the spiritual weapons God has given us to fight against the lies of the enemy. The first step toward this end is standing up and saying, "I recognize that this is a spiritual attack. The enemy wants to destroy me, but I'm not going to let him. Instead I'm going to use the sword of the Word of God to fight these lies and gain the victory."

• use the bible to recognize your true identity as God's daughter •

Shame tells you all the things that you are not. You're not pretty, educated, skinny, married, successful, and on and on and on. However, the truth of the Bible tells you who you are: First and foremost, you are God's chosen daughter, holy and beloved.

> *See what great love the Father has lavished on us, that we should be called children of God! And that is what we are! (1 John 3:1).*

> *Praise be to the God and Father of our Lord Jesus Christ, who has blessed us in the heavenly realms with every spiritual blessing in Christ. For he chose us in him before the creation of the world to be holy and blameless in his sight. In love he predestined us for adoption to sonship through Jesus Christ, in accordance with his pleasure and will—In him we were also chosen, having been predestined according to the plan of him who works out everything in conformity with the purpose of his will (Ephesians 1:3–5, 11).*

Because God chose us and adopted us, we are literally now daughters of the King of the universe. Even before you knew him, God chose you. He reached out to you. He made a way through his Son Jesus Christ for you to be adopted and become his daughter.

Notice this: God didn't choose you because of the things that you could or couldn't do. He was never interested in the lists of what you are or what you're not. He didn't choose you because of your abilities, your appearance, your education, your financial status, or your relationship status.

> *Brothers and sisters, think of what you were when you were called. Not many of you were wise by human standards; not many were influential; not many were of noble birth. But God chose the foolish things of the*

world to shame the wise; God chose the weak things of the world to shame the strong. God chose the lowly things of this world and the despised things—and the things that are not—to nullify the things that are (1 Corinthians 1:26–28).

So what is the antidote to the lies of the enemy when shame wants to list all the things that you are lacking? Well, it's to agree, with a twist.

The twist is that God doesn't care.

Even before you knew him, God chose you, and made a way through his Son Jesus Christ for you to be adopted and become his daughter. And even knowing all your faults and flaws, shortcomings and weaknesses, he still chose you and said, "I know what she's not. But if she will surrender herself to me and let me mold her into the image of my Son, Jesus Christ, and if she will obey me and follow the path I've laid out for her life—I am going to do amazing things with her life. Things that NOBODY could imagine. I'm not only going to revolutionize her life but I'm going to use her to start a revolution in my kingdom."

In ourselves, we really are nothing, but Jesus specializes in taking nothing and using it to bring glory to himself.

That's why one of the best ways to fight an attack of shame is to come back with: "I may not be all of the things you are listing, but God doesn't care. He still chose me to be his daughter, and he still has a plan to fulfill in my life."

• getting to the root of the problem •

Whenever enemies declare war, they always start by finding areas that are the most vulnerable to attack—the weaknesses. One thing I've learned in my own life is that in my battle with shame, Satan always attacks in my weakest areas—where I'm most vulnerable. That's why one of the keys to winning the battle against shame is getting to the root of the problem, dealing with it, and shoring up the weak areas.

For instance, in my own effort to overcome shame, I've had to face some issues in my past that created vulnerable areas in my soul and mind. On my journey, I've had to face the pain of rejection and abuse from my dad, and how his issues with women had a negative effect on my life. What I discovered is that one of the reasons being single was such a vulnerable area for me is because my dad tied my type-A personality (which he didn't like) to whether or not any man would ever want me. I have clear memories of him telling me, "If you don't change, no man is ever going to want you."

Even though it was God's plan for me to be single at this time, shame used my dad's words and the emotional pain that his words caused to create feelings of guilt, embarrassment, unworthiness, and disgrace. The only way I could overcome my issues with shame was to face my past, forgive my dad, and realize that his words were skewed by his own issues from his past. Then, I had to accept the truth that God is in control of my life, that he created me just the way I am, and that he has a unique plan and purpose for my life.

Now I know that as long as I am living in God's plan and purpose, being single is no longer a source of shame. In fact, after two years of having God heal the pain of my past and help me find my identity and purpose in him, I was able to return to that same conference and advertise For a Single Purpose—a ministry dedicated to ministering to single women.

What a dramatic change—from hiding in shame to using what I've learned to help other women! Still, I know this never would have been possible if I hadn't faced the source of my shame and applied biblical principles to the root of my problem.

That's why I encourage you—if you're struggling with shame, allow the Holy Spirit to heal the root of the problem in your life. If you need to go to a counselor to deal with your issues, then do it.

Don't allow shame to control you. Instead, take control of it by going to the root and tearing it out, saying, "You're not going to control my life any longer. I will be free!"

• accept God's forgiveness and new life •

Another big weapon the enemy uses to attack God's daughters with shame is reminding them of the sins of their past. Instead of reminding you of what you are not, he reminds you of what you were, with lies like:

"There's no way you can serve God with your history."

"How do you ever expect to be used by God after what you've done or after what you've lived through?"

"You're never going to overcome this area of your life. It's going to haunt you and plague you for the rest of your life—you'll never be free. You might as well just give up now."

Again, the goal is to get you to stop moving forward in obedience with God's plan for your life—and instead wallow in the chains of your past.

Once again—the key to overcoming is recognizing that this is a lie and choosing to fight shame with the truth of God's Word.

Therefore, if anyone is in Christ, the new creation has come: The old has gone, the new is here! (2 Corinthians 5:17).

Forget the former things; do not dwell on the past. See, I am doing a new thing! Now it springs up; do you not perceive it? I am making a way in the wilderness and streams in the wasteland (Isaiah 43:18-19).

Look at this truth from Romans 8:31-34:

What shall we say about such wonderful things as these? If God is for us, who can ever be against us? Since he did not spare even his own Son but gave him up for us all, won't he also give us everything else? Who dares accuse us whom God has chosen for his own? No one—for God himself has given us right standing with himself. Who then will condemn us? No one—for Christ Jesus died for us and was raised to life for us, and he is sitting in the place of honor at God's right hand, pleading for us.

No matter what happened in your past, you are not living there anymore. If you have repented and God has forgiven you, you're wholeheartedly following Jesus and allowing him to shape you into his image, then in God's eyes, the past is forgotten. When he looks at you now, he sees the blood of Jesus paid at Calvary. That's what it means to be justified—in God's eyes, it is just as if you have never sinned.

Because of this fact, Satan has no right to use the weapon of shame against you. You are a new creation, living a new life.

That may have been who you were...but it is not who you are now. If you want to overcome shame, you need to accept Christ's forgiveness, forgive yourself for the past, and claim your new identity as God's daughter, living your life for his glory.

• **if you really want to defeat shame once and for all, share your testimony** •

John 4 tells the story of the woman at the well. When we first meet her, she is absolutely covered with shame. Her shame had driven her into isolation—so much so that we meet her on her way to the well during the hottest, hardest time of day. It was the worst time of day to fetch water, but the only way that she could be sure she'd avoid people and hide in shame.

Then she had an encounter with Jesus. This encounter changed her life. He offered her something she desperately needed—a way to change her life—to be free from her shame and start all over again. Although she initially wanted the *living water* that he offered, in the end, she accepted the *new life* he gave when he told her that he was the Messiah.

That's when we see the most amazing thing happen. The conversation ends when the disciples return with the food. However, the story is not ending but taking a dramatic turn because somewhere during this woman's encounter with Jesus, she experienced a revolution.

Now instead of hiding in shame, she's actually going back into the town, seeking people out.

Rather than avoiding people because of her past, she's telling everyone who will listen, "I just met a man who told me everything I've ever done—he's the Messiah."

Because of the encounter that she had with Jesus Christ, her life was revolutionized. What was formerly her shame was now her testimony as she fulfilled the plan that God had for her life—becoming the catalyst for a revival in her town.

Over the years, fighting my own battle with shame, one thing I've learned is that whenever I choose to share the testimony of what Christ has done in my life, whenever I allow Christ to take the weak areas of my life and use them for his glory, shame has to run and hide.

Why? Because all of shame's power is lost when you decide to come out of hiding, tell the truth, admit your area of weakness, and say, "Let the parts of my life that Satan wants to fill with shame and use to devour me and my future, let them become a testimony of your faithfulness, of your mercy, of your power to intervene and bring life and freedom. God, if you can do anything with the ashes of my life, then feel free to make them beautiful."

As I shared with you before, years ago, my father's hurtful words and attempts at distorting and controlling my personality were causing me to be filled with shame because I was single.

I'm thankful the story doesn't end there. Instead, the story continued as God healed the broken areas of my life and helped me find my true identity and purpose in him.

In November 2014, I returned to the same conference, this time using my own testimony as a single Christian woman to start a ministry designed to encourage, inspire, and challenge single women. What a difference!

I hope this chapter inspires you to believe that shame can be overcome! Whatever its source, whatever role it's playing in your life, if you apply these steps to your own life, the Holy Spirit will be faithful and will deliver you from shame if you will cooperate with him and fight.

Freedom from shame is possible. I encourage you to start taking steps in that direction today.

• • • ⬤ • • •

Dear Father in heaven, As I read this chapter about shame, I know exactly what she's talking about. You and I know exactly what things I'd like to keep hidden, what vulnerable areas are most open to attack, and how often I'd like to shrink into a corner and hide. However, I don't want to live that way anymore. Starting today, I want to live in freedom. Just like the woman at the well, I want my deepest shame to become my greatest testimony.

From today on, let the parts of my life that Satan wants to fill with shame and use to devour me and my future, let them become a testimony of your faithfulness, of your mercy, of your power to intervene and bring life and freedom. God, if you can do anything with the ashes of my life, then feel free to make them beautiful. In Jesus' name, amen.

• the next step •

1. what things cause shame in your life?

2. do you accept shame as normal or look at it as a spiritual battle?

3. what is the root cause of your shame? are you willing to face it and overcome it?

4. what are some proactive steps you can take to help yourself understand your true identity as God's daughter?

5. has your life ever been changed by someone's willingness to overcome shame and share his or her testimony?

6. what could Jesus do with your life if you allowed him to turn your deepest shame into your greatest testimony?

chapter 9 • adessa

choosing contentment

As Robert Frost said:
> Two roads diverged in a wood, and I—
> I took the one less traveled by,
> And that has made all the difference.

Choices.

Decisions.

Our destination is based on the roads that we choose to take.

The choice to surrender our lives fully to God is the road that will lead to joy, peace, fulfillment, and satisfaction in life.

Another road that will lead to the same destination is the decision to choose contentment. This is an important key to being a happy single woman. Actually, it's one of the keys to being a happy woman, married or single.

Still, as a forty-year-old Christian single woman I completely understand the temptation to read a paragraph like that and think, "Easier said than done."

Seriously, I get it.

The good news is that so does every other person who was ever serious about the commitment to surrender his or her life completely to God. Everyone who's ever been there and done that knows that surrender doesn't just magically happen.

It isn't natural; it isn't normal. You can't just pray a prayer and instantly never want your own way again. (Too bad, because that would be so much easier.)

Instead, finding joy through surrender comes at the price of daily decisions to lay down your desires, your plans, and your ideas, and choosing to walk in obedience to God.

Sometimes the choice is filled with pain, and you have to choose to endure.

Other times the intensely human part of you rises up like a spoiled little child screaming, "I WANT MY OWN WAY!" and the spiritual part of you needs to rise up, take a stand, and say, "NO! Scream all you want but the answer is still NO."

There will be moments when you'll get a bad case of the "I deserves" and even times when you'll be tempted to feel "That's not fair."

The naked truth about surrender is that it's a constant struggle to prioritize your love for God over your love for yourself.

That's not always pretty; nor is it always easy. Even when you think you've got it licked, there will be days when you have to force yourself to once again choose: I will surrender my will to God's will and make good choices. You'll look in the mirror and say, "I can't believe I'm still struggling with this issue," only to realize you've only got one option: Surrender again and tell your flesh to DIE ALREADY.

It happened to me just this Christmas.

Yes, can you believe it, this Christmas—2014?!

Jennie and I had just started the online magazine part of For a Single Purpose, and every week we were writing articles encouraging women to enjoy their lives and their holidays when, for the first time in quite a while, I started feeling a tug toward discontentment. God was challenging me to overcome some difficult issues with my father when my brain went back to its natural default setting of "Life would be so much easier if I were married."

Let's be honest: The holidays are a difficult time to be single. In general, everything seems to be geared toward families. Television is bombarded with cheesy romantic movies where every problem is solved by falling in love. The very element of nostalgia and remembering Christmas past often reminds you that this wasn't the way you ever intended your life to go.

Then I got a phone call from a relative who hadn't contacted us in years. Of course, it didn't take long for her to ask the question, "So do you have a boyfriend yet?"

Even though I tried to answer the question in a way that was upbeat and positive and tell her that I'm really happy with my life, her reply was, "Well, that's what matters, that you're happy."

Now, I know that on paper this sounds like a kind response, but it wasn't.

I knew that response and I knew that tone of voice. It was the same response she'd give to a woman who was overweight when she'd say, "Well, at least you're healthy." Sigh.

It was pity, condescension, and criticism all rolled into one compact sentence.

Then it happened again. My brother and I were at a public function, having dinner with a couple we'd never met before. As we were getting to know each other, someone said, "So at your age, you've just never really found the right person?"

How do you even answer that?

I just smiled and said, "No, not yet."

Still, by the time the holiday wrapped up, I was starting to understand exactly why online dating services advertise so much in January. I remember saying to my brother, "It would be really easy for me to slide into a very depressed state right now—except that my life is just too full and good that I don't have the time."

It was an odd feeling.

On the one hand, I felt the pull to slip into my old pattern of feeling sorry for myself, discontent with my life, and angry with God that another holiday had passed and I was still single.

On the other side of the coin, I could feel the pull of the Holy Spirit inside saying, "Don't go there…look at all God is doing in your life and skip the pity party. Move past the holiday and continue following God."

Once again my flesh and my spirit were having a battle. The winner would be determined by the choice I made.

There's a quote that says, "Life may not be the party we hoped for, but while we're here, we should dance."

In Philippians 4:11 Paul says it this way, "For I have learned to be content whatever the circumstances."

In their own way, they are both saying the same thing—this is the life God has chosen to give me; I might as well enjoy it.

Does this mean you should never be sad or lonely?

Of course not, that would be unrealistic. All single women have moments when they wish they were married. However, we need to choose to move past these moments and choose to enjoy our lives just as they are right now.

I'm not going to say this is always easy. It's hard to take a *que sara sara* attitude when your life isn't going the way you hoped or dreamed.

I'm sure the apostle Paul understood this. Think about where he was when he wrote these words. He was sitting in prison for committing no crime other than preaching about Jesus. I'm sure there were days that he longed to feel the sun on his face, to take a walk wherever he wanted, or to eat better food than he was given.

However, as Paul sat in prison he had two choices: he could wallow in self-pity and become bitter, or he could choose to be content and accept that God was allowing this in his life. He could waste his days wishing he weren't in jail, or he could use his time to write letters and encourage the churches. Paul's choice was to learn to be content.

This is a key phrase for the Christian single woman.

Paul learned to be content.

He taught his thoughts and his emotions to accept that this was God's will for his life.

He learned to stop focusing on what he wished his circumstances were, and to start making the most of each day in his circumstances.

This is a vital lesson for any woman who wants to follow God's will during her own stage of singleness. You need to accept that God has allowed you to be single at this time. Rather than wasting time feeling sorry for yourself, pouting, and punishing the world because you are unhappy, you need to accept God's plan and learn to be content where he's placed you.

Trust me, this is something you will have to teach yourself.

It's not going to come naturally. Contentment is something we have to force ourselves to "put on."

It's like getting up and getting dressed in the morning. Speaking only for myself, I can say that I look very different when I first get out of bed in the morning than I do when I leave the house. Quite frankly, my early morning self is not attractive.

When I first get up, my hair is a mess; there are pillow marks on my face and sleepy-eye gunk around my eyes. If I decided to go through my day looking like I did first thing in the morning, I think I'd turn a few heads. (Not in a good way, but more like, "Can you believe she left the house looking like that?")

Obviously, I make another choice.

I get up, wash my hair, brush my teeth, and make myself look better. Then I "put on" makeup, nice clean clothes, some jewelry, and choose how I'm going to look before I leave the house.

Trust me, my choice to put on better attire makes ALL THE DIFFERENCE.

Just like my decision to put my sleepy-time attire aside for the day and make myself more presentable to the world makes all the difference in my outward appearance, so our choice to "put on" contentment will make all the difference in every area of our lives.

Even though it may be more natural for us to wear an attitude of discontentment, jealousy, anger, or depression, choosing this road will ultimately lead us to a place that we don't want to go: The pit of self-pity. There are no happy or fulfilled citizens in that town—just sad, disgruntled malcontents wallowing in their own anger that things didn't turn out the way they had planned. What a tragedy!

The good news is that this does not have to be the end of any woman's story. We were not created to live our lives in the pit of self-pity. God has a much higher purpose in mind for each of his daughters. Whether or not we fulfill God's purpose for our lives or waste our lives in the pit of self-pity depends on the choices we make.

Will we choose surrender or selfishness?

Will we choose contentment or self-pity?

The choice is up to you.

At this point you may be saying, "Okay, I hear you, and I want to make positive choices. I want to put on contentment; I just don't know where to start."

Here are some practical steps to start teaching yourself to be content:

• stop focusing on what you want and thank God for what you have •

Give thanks in all circumstances; for this is God's will for you in Christ Jesus (1 Thessalonians 5:18).

When we focus on what we have to be thankful for, it changes our perspective and helps us to become more content. It may sound old-fashioned and corny, but there really is something to be said for "counting your blessings" as a way to change your attitude.

For example, over the holidays when I started feeling myself slipping into the pit of self-pity, I forced myself to start talking about all that God was doing in my life. As I focused on ministry opportunities that were coming up in January, the people God had placed in my life, and even the blessings he had provided, my attitude began to change. That's when I realized I couldn't fit a pity party into my schedule; there was too much living to do!

• choose to praise God •

When you feel yourself sinking into sadness, turn off the television, put down the romance novel and say "goodbye" to secular music. Instead, put on some praise music and start singing along. Put on the garment of praise to replace your spirit of heaviness (Isaiah 61:3). Follow Paul's example and choose to praise the Lord even in the most difficult of circumstances, and watch your attitude change!

• focus on being a blessing to someone else •

Nothing will change your attitude and help you experience contentment more than taking your eyes off your own situation and reaching out to help someone less fortunate than yourself. As the old saying goes, "I felt sorry for myself because I had no shoes until I saw a man who had no feet." It's all about perspective, and helping someone in a worse situation than you will change your perspective.

• accept that God knows best •

Okay, I'm not going to minimize this—I know some of you are facing truly challenging obstacles where it seems almost impossible to be content. You're suffering and you want out of these circumstances NOW. How can you learn to be content?

Let's look at Psalm 131 and take a lesson from King David—a man who was very familiar with heartache and difficult circumstances. It reads:

My heart is not proud, Lord, my eyes are not haughty; I do not concern myself with great matters or things too wonderful for me. But I have calmed and quieted myself, I am like a weaned child with its mother; like a weaned child I am content. Israel, put your hope in the Lord *both now and forevermore.*

Very much like the apostle Paul, David knew the key to being content was to be calm and accept the circumstances, quiet his soul, and put his hope in the Lord. He had fully submitted his will to God's will and relinquished the "I deserves" that come with a proud heart and the discontentment that comes with an envious heart. Instead, he chose to be humble and trust that God knows what he's doing and he will be content to live in God's will for his life.

Believe me when I say I know this is not easy. During many years of my life I chose the wrong road and was discontent with the path God chose for my life.

I wanted more. I thought I deserved more, and I envied those who had more.

Then the Holy Spirit convicted me of the sin of being discontent. He showed me that I had to stop envying other people's lives and begin enjoying and appreciating my own life. During that time I had to learn, like David, to quiet my soul and to be content.

At first, it wasn't easy. It never is when we're retraining our brains. However, looking back now I can honestly say that this "correction" was one of the greatest gifts God has ever given me because it taught me how to put on contentment.

Now when I'm feeling the pull toward discontentment or depression, I've learned that it's my responsibility to make a choice, take action, and put on contentment. Whenever I choose to follow Paul's footsteps and choose contentment, I can genuinely say that when the moment of temptation passes and I'm thinking clearly again, I am happy with what God has provided. I have learned that whatever God gives and wherever he leads, it's going to be pretty wonderful. Maybe not exactly what I planned, but still pretty wonderful.

So what about you?

Like the two roads that diverged in the woods, two choices stand before you: contentment or discontentment, joy or envy, thankfulness or ungratefulness. Which one will you choose?

Will you follow the path that leads to the pit of self-pity or will you choose to take the road less traveled and choose to fulfill the purpose God has for your life?

The choice is completely dependent on whether or not you will learn to be content.

• • • ⬬ • • •

Dear heavenly Father, I come to you in Jesus' name and ask you to forgive me for every time that I have been discontent, each time I've chosen the road that leads to self-pity, and every time I've followed my natural inclinations of selfishness and been a poor reflection of a Christian single woman. Please help me to daily choose to put on contentment. Help me to lay down my will and, like Paul, learn to be content in every situation through the power of Jesus Christ. Amen.

• the next step •

1. what do you currently do to find contentment in your everyday life?

2. a quote in the chapter said: "life may not be the party we hoped for, but while we're here, we should dance." how does your life reflect this?

3. how can we "learn" to be content? what are some specific choices you can make to help you "put on" contentment?

4. what are some steps you can take to actively find contentment in every day?

chapter 10 • jennie

choosing to not get stuck

*I*n this new journey of single life and single motherhood, I finally had reached a season where I began feeling as though I wasn't working so hard to simply survive. After two years of treading water just to stay above the waves and catch occasional breaths, I was starting to feel like I could rest a bit and breathe again with less difficulty and struggle. The stormy sky began to part and reveal brighter days and the steady waves of challenges had calmed.

peace.

I was looking forward to establishing some new traditions that Christmas with my daughter: baking cookies and decorating together, shopping, and attending holiday parties. I was embracing our new family unit of two and settling in to find joy in our every day. There were also some potential blessings hanging in the balance and I found myself looking forward.

hope.

And then WHAM!!! In a week's time all that I was looking forward to, hoping for, praying for, and planning for fell apart and I came UNDONE!

I had barely returned home and unpacked from a Thanksgiving trip to be with my family and I landed myself in the emergency room! Severe pain with an extremely quick onset had me driving myself (like a mad woman) to the hospital. Curbs were jumped; stop signs and red lights were suddenly just suggestions as I was doubling over.

After many hours and multiple tests at the hospital, I was told to go home, rest, and take my meds to render myself unconscious to keep the pain at bay until I could be scheduled for surgery sometime in the new year.

I sarcastically thought to myself, "That's EXACTLY what I had on my wish list this year! Another surgery!"

Coincidently, I had surgery the year before, right before Christmas, and spent the time sore and medicated. Oh, how I thought this year would be different. Better.

Unfortunately, this wasn't the only thing that derailed my week and subsequently my thought process and emotions. On top of this abrasive new reality landed a disappointment that even now, a while later, leaves me still trying to figure out and understand the hows and whys.

Sometimes we are handed things that we aren't meant to handle and figure out on our own. This is where the enemy likes to step in and cause you to question your hope, rob your peace, and demolish any joy you thought you had or ever would have.

Once your mind starts taking a trip to Doomsville, every little thing that creeps up becomes overwhelming and can turn on the waterworks or stir frustration and anger in seconds. The rest of my week became a "Series of Unfortunate Events" which, by the grace of God, I can now look back at with a little humor. However, in the moment, not so much!

Throughout that week, I was trying to manage pain, extreme nausea, doctor visits and scheduling, random fevers, and still care for my daughter. I was exhausted, miserable, disappointed, and feeling sorry for myself. Two days after my eventful trip to the ER, I woke up in the morning just knowing that was the day the pity party was happening. I was just sad and in my sadness, ridiculousness ensued!

I made the effort, that morning, to make some coffee and get something to eat (which took a lot out of me). I managed to drop my plate of food and half of my eggs suddenly became a scavenger hunt for my two cats. I cut my losses, headed to the couch with now one (severely) scrambled egg and cup of coffee and prepared to get situated comfortably (this also felt like work).

Just as I found the optimum position to sit and eat in minimal pain, I picked up my coffee. As I went to sip, I realized the cup was nowhere near my mouth as the hot liquid poured all down the front of me!

Later that day, a friend came to help with some things around the house. While she was here, I managed to cut my finger on the kitchen countertop. Don't ask! These things just happen and it's always nonsensical. But it was a very deep cut that took a long time to stop bleeding and just layered more pain on top of existing pain.

That evening, my stomach took a sudden turn as a result of taking pain meds. I cannot quite describe the thoughts and feelings that one experiences when the toilet you are desperate for is found clogged with an excessive amount of toilet paper and water is filled to the brim and not draining. I love my little girl, but oh my! I did not have the physical ability to be patient in that moment. I also faced the daunting reality that we did not own a plunger!

Desperate times call for desperate measures!

I quickly grabbed whatever random household products I could find to help break up the wads of paper. Drano, baking soda, and vinegar were all dumped in. Result: lots of bubbles but no breakthrough. My daughter and I went on a rapid hunt through the house for long-stemmed items that could help us on our quest. In case you find yourself in a similar predicament, crow bars and mini-blind open-closer wands do NOT work to unclog a toilet. The classic and unfailing toilet brush came through for me that evening and is, I'm happy to report, cheap enough to replace.

Needless to say, after the day that I had and especially the final episode, I was EXHAUSTED and feeling quite sore. The final thing I attempted to do was take a nearly empty plastic lemonade container out of the fridge to be washed. Just as I picked it up I dropped it on the hard tile floor and a huge chunk of the pitcher cracked like glass and the remaining contents spilled and splashed everywhere. I was SO DONE!!

I could barely bend down to clean up the mess and throw my container away. I just needed to sit, rest, and not touch another thing in the house.

I fixed myself a cup of tea (which I spilled a good portion of on the kitchen floor I had just cleaned) and went directly toward my favorite spot on the couch. As I removed my slippers, sat down, and propped my feet up, my cat came over and vomited inside my slipper!

So we're not giving up. How could we! Even though on the outside it often looks like things are falling apart on us, on the inside, where God is making new life, not a day goes by without his unfolding grace (2 Corinthians 4:16 The Message).

The following week I had friends come to help my daughter and me decorate for Christmas. They made our home feel warm and cozy and our hearts full. I had been disappointed I wasn't going to be able to physically do this, but receiving their help made me realize how blessed I was to have them in my life.

The night before they arrived, another friend brought dinner and came to clean and prep my house for decorating day. This friend also helped us to do our usual Christmas cookie baking that I was afraid my daughter and I would miss out on.

There were several others who made us meals or came to help. They made us realize how genuinely loved we truly are. Friends, sometimes you don't realize who and what there is around you until you find yourself in a pit!

Navigating through those dark, lonely places is where we find God's grace, provision, and rest. Without them, we would never have a need for it and never learn how to tap into it. In our desperation, if we are looking in the right place and surrender ourselves before the Lord, we can actually see and experience his blessings.

love.

I am personally aware that many are struggling to connect with the world around them because they're weighed down and buried under the disappointments and pressures of life. As I mentioned earlier, I faced a series of difficult experiences in a short period of time that started to lead me down a very dangerous emotional path. Too many disappointing and stressful things to process at once can often lead to an overload of thoughts and feelings that bog us down. I got caught up into the downward spiral of negative thinking and sadness. What I learned this time, as I was sinking into the pit of despair, was how to recognize when you're on your way down and what to do to climb back out.

I knew the moment I woke up one morning that I was going to have an unscheduled pity party. I was able to tell from the tone of my thoughts.

Immediately I knew that, like any good party…

• it's best if you invite friends •

Not to join me in my misery, but to pray for me as I began my pouting session. I have an arsenal of prayer warriors that, at the words "please pray," they are on it! No questions asked. Align yourself with such people.

Be such a person. And learn to immediately use them in moments such as these. Recognize that when life begins to happen to us, we can't often handle it on our own and we need to call in reinforcements.

• a good pity party also requires a really good venting session •

You need to process those emotions and *let them out!* What you are feeling is typically valid and justifiable. But I've learned the hard way that not everyone can handle the heavy emotions of others. The key is finding a safe place to vent. For some, the safest place may be a journal.

I am blessed to have a friend who will let me text crazy rants throughout the day. She will check in with me later to see how I'm processing it all and provide perspective when needed. Most of the time, she knows I just need to get it out and doesn't feel the need to adjust my emotions. Such a friend is a rare and true gift. I will just tell you that reading back through the string of texts I sent during my pity party was almost entertaining, and I'm sure she laughs at me half of the time. Until you find one of these friends, learn to be one of these friends.

• every party needs good music •

Music has the ability to set a tone and mood for those listening, so choose wisely. If you can sense the emotional downward spiral beginning, make the difficult choice to fill your home and your heart with praise to God. You may not feel like it, but we can't operate through life based on our feelings. Sometimes we need to take steps in the right direction and make conscious decisions to adjust our thought process and emotions. Be intentional to list all of the things that are right or okay in your life; things you can be grateful for. There has to be something! If you have a radio or CD player to listen to or a device to read books and articles on, you have something tangible to be thankful for.

With perspective and a WHOLE lot of prayer, I was pulled out of that yucky pit and stopped seeing all that I was losing and lacking. I started to readjust my sights onto what I still had right in front of me and was able to find strength to praise God for that.

It's hard to praise at a pity party; I'm not going to lie. The mindset has to change and what you're uttering must shift from complaints to gratitude. But I can tell you from personal experience that it can be done.

> *When you go through deep waters, I will be with you. When you go through rivers of difficulty, you will not drown. When you walk through the fire of oppression, you will not be burned up; the flames will not consume you. For I am the* Lord, *your God, the Holy One of Israel, your Savior (Isaiah 43:2–3 NLT).*

Dear heavenly Father, I know that you are with me during all seasons of my life. I know that you see me and you care for me when I am coming undone and life appears to be falling apart. You see when every tear falls and when I've reached emotional exhaustion. I invite you to attend all of my pity parties in the future. I know that you will be faithful to carry me through them and not get stuck. I do not want the negative things in my life to render me ineffective for you and your purposes. I trust that you will bring women into my life to embrace me during that time and help me to develop a plan that will keep my focus on you during those overwhelming moments and seasons. Thank you for your grace. In Jesus' name, amen.

• the next step •

1. list as many close women friends as you can that you could connect with as "silent" prayer partners, people you know that will pray with you when you simply say "please pray!" no questions asked. (approach a few before a need arises and share your idea. be sure to offer the same benefit to them.)

living for a single purpose

2. to whom or where do you go to vent when you need to unload heavy emotions? has this been a safe and effective form of venting?

3. what may be some more productive avenues to process some of the deep things in your heart?

4. set up your playlist for your next pity party. make sure it's all music that is going to turn your focus to God and will fill your home with praise even if it takes your heart and mind a bit to catch up.

5. MAKE A PLAN: plan out your next pity party. when the cloud of negative perspective starts to settle on your mind, know the "who, what, and where" for your party so you can keep it brief and effective!

chapter 11 • jennie

choosing true love

love.

As a single woman, sometimes hearing or seeing that word stings. We all desire to be loved, cherished, and adored. We long for someone to see beauty and value in us. We want to be validated, encouraged, and cared for. And for some wackadoo reason, we think that a MAN is the only way this can happen! I'm not sure whether we can blame society or Hallmark, but somewhere along our journey we've adopted the belief that this is truth.

We tend to live in constant disappointment when our reality doesn't line up with what we believe is true. It's almost as though our value or purpose in life is expected to be driven by a whimsical, magical romantic adventure. Without it, our lives are considered meaningless and flat. This false belief must be addressed and combated with truth.

Often the sense that something is missing is a reflection of the failure to realize what we *have* or what *is*.

We feel as though we are not enough. That we don't have what it takes to be completely wonderful and whole all on our own.

That our lives are not significant and valuable without a significant other who values us.

That we are unable to speak into and bless those around us with the little we have to offer.

I'd like to remind you that God does his best work with situations that appear to be *not enough*. Too few loaves and fish, empty oil jars, shortage of wine, illness, death; these are what he tends to use to reveal the depths of his love and genuine care for our individual needs. He can use whatever we have to offer him and do more with us than we could ever imagine.

Allow God to bring you to a place of wholeness in him during this season of singleness. If you are able to live a whole and fulfilled life alone, the joy and bonus of having someone to share it with will be an added blessing. You will relieve that person from the responsibility of meeting your needs, and you will be less likely to be disappointed in your marriage as well.

Seek out truth for your value and identity in Christ. Choose to hear God's heart and perspective of you. Meditate on it daily until you've replaced every false belief about yourself and you are living your life with the freedom of knowing your worth.

• we are loved by our heavenly Father •

See what great love the Father has lavished on us, that we should be called children of God! And that is what we are! (1 John 3:1).

• we are forgiven •

You, Lord, are forgiving and good, abounding in love to all who call to you (Psalm 86:5).

• we have hope •

Let us hold unswervingly to the hope we profess, for he who promised is faithful (Hebrews 10:23).

• we are beautiful •

I praise you because I am fearfully and wonderfully made; I know that full well (Psalm 139:14).

• we were created on purpose •

For we are God's handiwork, created in Christ Jesus to do good works, which God prepared in advance for us to do (Ephesians 2:10).

By believing God's truth about ourselves, we are able to see what doesn't line up with that in the world around us. Our perspective will shift and we will recognize where our beliefs were skewed in the past.

When we find ourselves laden with disappointment, fear, lack, and anxiety about what we see in our lives, go back to the Word of God and meditate on what is true. It takes habitual training to take a step back from certain situations and glean from the Lord before reacting or responding. Keep practicing. You won't get it right every time. We are certainly not perfect, but we can take daily steps in the right direction.

Over time, you will develop a clear understanding of God's love for you, his purpose for you and how he sees his cherished daughter. You will begin to walk in the confidence of this truth and realize that all the validation, affirmation, acceptance, and love you ever needed comes from God. You will see your value through his eyes and understand his purpose for your life without needing the influence or opinion of another person.

• • • ⬤ • • •

The Valentine's Day (otherwise known as Single's Awareness Day) immediately following my ex-husband's departure was, by far, one of the worst I've ever experienced. The holiday seemed to amplify my feelings of rejection, pain, and loss with all the commercialism of romance and emphasis on relationships. I was faced with some very important decisions during that season that would determine how I walked out my journey. To be quite honest, hiding in my bedroom at my parents' house, remaining in my jammies for days on end while eating ice cream and sulking was definitely my most natural choice of response and the first that came to mind. However, I was able to think forward a bit to realize the waste of time and lack of effectiveness this would have on my life. I was determined to rise above the mess and not let it turn me into something and someone I never desired to be.

I was also acutely aware that my daughter was watching my every move. She was going to learn how to walk through adversity with grace and peace, but only if I showed her. With each day that I chose to get out of bed, every moment I pressed in to build relationships and interact with others, I was being watched. I came to realize that it wasn't just my daughter observing my choice to consistently cling to God, but family and friends were also paying close attention.

I suppose enough people have seen a marriage crumble before their eyes to have certain assumptions as to how most usually handle the collapse. They also know how they would probably handle the same betrayal and rejection that I had been subject to, and this typically includes the "Recluse Response" of jammies and ice cream. So, when they would see me out and about with my make-up on and my hair brushed, I received many shocked responses. Some were actually quite comical.

I knew as Valentine's Day was approaching that I needed to be proactive in how I addressed the pending doom or potential wave of heartache of this day. I decided immediately that I wasn't going to tackle it alone! I had connected with two single women at my parents' church since I had moved back home and was pretty sure they had no desire to be alone that evening either.

I invited them over for an "All Things Red" dinner. The three of us collaborated on the meal and each made special red treats to munch on throughout the evening. One of the girls even picked up a video for us to watch. My daughter especially loved decorating for the evening and setting the table with the "fancy stuff Nana keeps in the cabinet." We made it our own special celebration. We talked, laughed, and for a while I was able to forget why I was even celebrating that evening without my husband.

I guess what I want to encourage you to do for Valentine's Day and every holiday is to embrace the moments that could potentially cause added pain or feelings of loss, and find ways to celebrate the people in your life that God has placed there for you to love. You may have siblings or parents, aunts, uncles, nieces, or nephews in your life that you can choose to pour your love into this season. Some of them may be a little more difficult to love than others or be super quirky and difficult to connect with, but seek God for special ways you can show them love. It doesn't have to be some grand gesture or cause financial strain to make a point. It may just be a sacrifice of time or energy to be present in their lives and embrace times together as family.

If you don't live in close proximity to your immediate family, or if it's necessary for you to limit time with them due to dysfunction, then choose to get involved in your local church and create a family there. And remember—you have to be a friend to make a friend! Just because you're the new girl doesn't mean you can't be the one inviting people over or initiating a get-together. Get involved in some group or area to serve to connect with others right away. Start to open your eyes to see the world and people around you.

If you stop and think about it (and maybe even make a list), there are probably numerous people that you can truly share God's love with at this time in your life. Without thinking of what or who you are lacking, embrace those right in front of you.

Here are some practical suggestions on how you can make loving and showing love to others your primary focus on Valentine's Day and all year round.

- **Send flowers to a friend at work to brighten her day**
- **Do a gift exchange with your single friends**
- **Plan a night out and get dressed up**
- **Schedule a movie night and get a bunch of friends together to either stay in or go out**
- **Send an encouraging card or letter**
- **Host a fancy dinner party for friends or family**
- **Buy gifts or make up food baskets for those in need around the holidays**
- **Plan a cookie-baking day around Christmas with your mom or sister or friend**

I'm sure if you tap into your creativity you'll be able to come up with many more. Collaborate with your friends and family and come up with some great ways to show each other that you value their place in your life.

Whatever you do, choose to enjoy life and the lives of those around you. Choose to see your blessings and not your lack. Choose to bless others in spite of your own feelings. Choose to celebrate love.

And…choose to only eat ice cream in your jammies if you are hosting a slumber party and you have plenty of girlfriends or nieces and nephews to join you!

For those of you still struggling to embrace this season of life in a positive way, *Chin up!* There is no need to beat yourself up for feeling too sorry for yourself—this is counterproductive. There is also no need to stay in this sulky, feel-sorry-for-yourself state. Today, let's make a choice to not dwell on the past and let's embrace every positive element that is present in our daily lives.

This is not just true for our singleness, but it also rings true for every other scenario in life that falls short of what we hoped for.

> *Fix your thoughts on what is TRUE, and HONORABLE, and RIGHT, and PURE, and LOVELY, and ADMIRABLE. Think about things that are excellent and worthy of praise (Philippians 4:8 NLT, emphasis mine).*

We need to be intentional to think of such things. Our minds get quickly clouded by all the negative that comes our way and we lose sight of what's good. Take a moment, today, to make a list of all the blessings right in front of you. I encourage you to do this often, especially if you struggle, as I do, to keep positive perspective of what we have.

This takes time and a bit of mental work to retrain your brain to see things in this light. When we dwell on all that's gone wrong or is going wrong, we can easily get our minds stuck there. In turn, we may fail to venture into a new opportunity out of fear.

We may find ourselves anxious about our future because we are still staring at our past.

We will stop encouraging those around us to be courageous because we've given up in our own fight.

What we choose to dwell on will directly affect our choices and actions.

If you are unable to see what is true, honorable, right, pure, lovely, and admirable, spend time in God's Word and let it be a daily reminder. Ask him for his perspective of people and situations. Write each of these items down along the left side of a sheet of paper and write next to each word something that you see in your life that is a reflection of these that you can dwell on and choose to see each day.

• • • ⬤ • • •

Dear Lord, today I bring to you all that I am and all that I lack. I know that you can make beautiful things out of dust and I trust you to do the same in my life. I choose to look to you as I seek to find my identity and discover who I am in you. Help me to see the beauty and the good in all that you've created. Help me to see myself and others the way you see us. May I reflect your love on those around me. Open my heart and mind so that I am able to love fully. I thank you for loving me even when I am unable to love myself. I praise you and I thank you for your faithfulness and goodness. In Jesus' name, amen.

• the next step •

1. what false beliefs have you adopted that have caused you to see yourself or your life as "less than"?

2. now look at those false beliefs and state what IS truth according to the word of God.

3. when you slip back into thinking these negatives about yourself, what can you do to recognize what is truth and how can you set your mind on that?

4. list the people in your life you would like to reach out to or connect with more.

5. what are the ways you plan to make this connection and what are some ways you can be a blessing to them?

chapter 12 • adessa

choosing to never settle

*H*ardly a week goes by that I don't hear the same old story. The names and circumstances always vary slightly, but the storyline remains the same. A Christian woman is tired of being single. She's had it with the loneliness, the lack of intimacy, and being alone in a world full of couples. She looked around the church, but for one reason or another she found no perspective partners. It wasn't long until her name is added to the list of Christian single women that have decided to settle for dating a non-Christian man rather than continue being alone.

My heart breaks every time I hear this story.

I heard it again today. A friend of mine was heartbroken because a woman close to her made the decision to begin dating a non-Christian. Although she didn't say it, I could hear in her voice that she wanted to grab her friend and say, "Don't you know that you're worth more than you're settling for?"

At least, that's what I usually feel like doing when I hear these stories over and over again.

It's my first response when I hear about a single mom settling for the first guy who came along, even though he isn't a Christian and has no interest in becoming a Christian.

It's on the tip of my tongue every time I listen to a Christian woman explaining why she's sleeping with her boyfriend even though she knows the Bible says it's a sin.

I want to shout it from the rooftops whenever I see any woman allowing herself or her children to be abused by a man who isn't even her husband. Not that any woman should accept abuse, but why would anyone stay in an abusive relationship when there is no legal commitment?

Why are the daughters of God, the princesses of our heavenly Father's kingdom, cheapening their value and allowing themselves to be treated like second-rate citizens?

The only conclusion I can find is that deep inside, they don't know what they are worth. Perhaps one reason that they struggle to comprehend their value is that they are searching for their significance and value in the wrong place. They're looking for a man to make them feel valuable, when they need to be looking into the eyes of their heavenly Father.

Please, my dear sisters, don't think that as I am writing this that I do not understand your struggle. Every woman has a craving inside of her for the love of a husband and family. Most women are blessed to experience these relationships at some point in their lives. However, it was never God's will that these relationships define your value. And it is not God's will that these cravings ever dominate your heart and your mind to the degree that they cause you to disobey God's explicit laws laid out in the Bible.

Let me be clear: God has made several commands regarding dating and relationships in the Bible. If you are disobeying these commands then you are sinning and choosing a relationship with a man over your relationship with God.

2 Corinthians 6:14–18 says,

Do not be yoked together with unbelievers. For what do righteousness and wickedness have in common? Or what fellowship can light have with darkness? What harmony is there between Christ and Belial? Or what does a believer have in common with an unbeliever? What agreement is there between the temple of God and idols? For we are the temple of the living God. As God has said:

"I will live with them and walk among them, and I will be their God, and they will be my people."

Therefore, "Come out from them and be separate," says the Lord. "Touch no unclean thing, and I will receive you."

And, "I will be a Father to you, and you will be my sons and daughters, says the Lord Almighty."

1 Corinthians 6:18–20 says,

Flee from sexual immorality. All other sins a person commits are outside the body, but whoever sins sexually, sins against their own body. Do you not know that your bodies are temples of the Holy Spirit, who is in you, whom you have received from God? You are not your own; you were bought at a price. Therefore honor God with your bodies.

The Bible is explicit: Single Christians should not date non-Christians; and for Christians, sex is to be exclusively reserved for those who are married. These verses are very clear.

But did you notice while you were reading these verses that God explains why he wants his children to obey these commands? Each time, he places our value as his children as the reason we should be selective about who we choose to date and how we act in a dating relationship.

Let's take another look at 1 Corinthians 6:18–20.

Do you not know that your bodies are temples of the Holy Spirit, who is in you, whom you have received from God? You are not your own; you were bought at a price. Therefore honor God with your bodies.

These verses say that because the Holy Spirit lives inside of you, your body is literally the temple of God. Your body doesn't belong to you any longer—it belongs to God. When God looks at you, he doesn't see your height, your weight, any hidden gray hairs, laugh lines, or wrinkles. He sees a body that is housing the Holy Spirit. Whenever we use our bodies to sin or gratify the desires of our flesh, we are defying the Holy Spirit that lives inside of us.

Think of it this way: You shouldn't be doing anything on a date that you wouldn't be comfortable doing at the altar of your church or the foot of the cross.

That may sound silly to some people, but that's because we've got things mixed up. We see the altar at our church as a holy place, but the truth is that it's our very bodies that are a holy place. Even though we live in a culture that equates our bodies with sexuality, God says our bodies are meant to be holy houses where the Holy Spirit can dwell and function. When you see yourself and your body through God's eyes instead of the eyes of this culture, you will realize you are worth so much more than you settle for.

Let's move a little further down in this verse:

You are not your own; you were bought at a price. Therefore honor God with your bodies.

Sometimes, as Christians, the gospel story becomes so familiar and redundant to us that we forget the incredible price that Jesus paid when he came to earth and died on the cross so that we could have forgiveness of sins, restored fellowship with God, and the promise of eternity in heaven. But let's take a moment and remember.

Do you remember what your life was like before Jesus rescued you? Perhaps you've been raised in the church all of your life and you've never known anything else. Then take a look around you at your unsaved friends and family. Talk to your parents or grandparents, or whatever generation remembers not walking with Jesus. Find out what your life would be like if it weren't for the incredible mercy of Jesus.

Remember that you aren't entitled to grace—it was a gift. You were entitled and destined for judgment, destruction, complete alienation from God in this life, reaping the consequences of all of your sinful choices, and spending an eternity in hell. This was going to be your reality until Jesus intervened and saved you. In fact, this is why we call it "saved," because you were rescued from all these things.

You are where you are today not because of anything you did, but because your heavenly Father loved you so much that he sent his one and only Son into the world to die a hideous, torturous, humiliating death to pay the price for your sins. Now, because of what he did on the cross, you are no longer God's enemy that is destined for judgment, but you are his precious daughter whom he loves.

When he looks at you, he sees the blood of Jesus covering your sins, and the Holy Spirit living inside of you. Because of this, he says, "You were worth the blood of my Son; don't settle for less and dishonor him or yourself."

Let's move up to 2 Corinthians 6:16-18,

"I will live with them and walk among them, and I will be their God, and they will be my people."

Therefore, "Come out from them and be separate, says the Lord. Touch no unclean thing, and I will receive you."

And, "I will be a Father to you, and you will be my sons and daughters, says the Lord Almighty."

In the first set of verses, we are reminded of our value as the temple of the Holy Spirit and as souls who were bought with a price. However, in these verses, God tells us that we are valuable because of our personal relationship with him.

He starts by reminding us that we are his people. We belong to him.

As women, we tend to derive our identity from our relationships. We're somebody's daughter, somebody's wife, or somebody's mother. When our lives are missing these relationships, we tend to lose our identity and feel worthless or invaluable. That's when we start settling for anybody so that we can feel like somebody.

My dear sisters in Christ, it is time this pattern changed. Whether you are a wife, a girlfriend, a mother, or not, if you are a Christian, you always have an identity, you always have value, and you always have worth.

Yes, your value is tied to a relationship—your relationship with God. Whether or not you are with a man, God needs to be the one who fills your needs. He is the one who will walk with you every day and live with you all the time. He is the one who will fill the needs you have to be beautiful, validated, treasured, and loved. After he has filled those needs, then you will start seeing yourself as the treasure that you are, and stop settling for relationships that are outside of God's will.

There may be some women who are reading this book and saying, "But Adessa, this is all well and good. You've made your point and got all your theology right, but you don't understand how I FEEL. I need someone to give me the love I've never had in my life. Starting with my father, all of my relationships with men have been messed up, and I am sick of feeling unlovable. I want to be loved, and valued and treasured and I want it now!"

I'll be honest with you, I understand that a lot of the reasons women settle for relationships and men that are not God's will and not healthy have to do with their unresolved father issues. Even while I'm writing these words, the heavenly Father and I are discussing some of my own unresolved issues with my dad. There are times when I'm so frustrated with our relationship that I think, "I wish I could just get married and know what it is like to feel loved and valued."

Whenever I hear those words flowing through my mind or coming from my mouth, I know it's time to stop and reconnect with my heavenly Father. This isn't the time for a pity party or to go on a wild manhunt, searching for someone to fill the needs my father left in my soul. It's time to go to my heavenly Father and once again allow him to refill my soul with his love, his approval, his validation. It's time for me to curl up in his arms and remember that I'm God's daughter, and as such I have value, I have worth, and I am deeply loved and cared for. In these quiet moments, I remember that I don't want to settle for anything less than my heavenly Father's absolute best for my life. Together, we move forward again.

You see, so often as Christian singles we read the verses that say, "Don't date non-Christians" and "Abstain from all sexual activity until marriage" and we think, "God just doesn't understand." But nothing could be further from the truth.

He does understand.

He understands why you're even tempted to settle for a life and a relationship that you don't really want. (Let's face it, Christian single women want to marry godly single men and raise godly families—we may settle for less, but deep inside we really want the best.)

Even while we're being told who not to date and what not to do, the Bible, God's Word to us, is telling us why not to do it: because you're worth more than that.

You're worth more than a relationship with a non-believer who will constantly challenge your faith and cause you to question your own commitment to Christ.

You're worth more than a one-night stand or even an ongoing sexual relationship with no commitment attached.

You're worth more than being the mistress to someone else's husband.

You have been bought with the precious, holy blood of Jesus.

You have the Holy Spirit of God living inside of you.

You have a personal relationship with the God who created the universe.

God Almighty calls YOU his daughter—the King of heaven says YOU are his princess.

You are worth more than you settle for.

Today is the day to stop settling and claim your rightful identity as a daughter of God and find your true identity in him.

• • • ⬬ • • •

Dear heavenly Father, you know me so much better than I know myself. You know each and every longing of my heart and ache in my soul. You know my past and my present and understand better than I do why I choose to settle for things that are not in your perfect will for my life. Father, I ask that today you would help me to change and make better choices. I ask that you would first of all help me to find my identity and worth in you so that I stop settling for relationships that promise to fill my desires but only leave me empty and further from you in the end. Lord, I ask you to forgive me for each time I've sinned and chosen to settle rather than obey the Bible. Forgive me for each time I've defiled my body—your temple. From this day forward, I commit myself to living as a holy, godly woman before you. I will not settle for anything less than your perfect will and your ways in my life. Please help me to keep my commitment. In Jesus' name, amen.

• the next step •

1. in what ways have you settled in the past?

2. are you ever tempted to take God's grace for granted? what would your life be like if God hadn't intervened?

3. do you tend to base your value on your human relationships or your relationship with God?

4. what changes are you going to make to reflect your unwillingness to settle?

chapter 13 • adessa

choosing to not be a desperate female hunter

The other day I was watching *The Andy Griffith Show*. It was one of my favorite episodes. For those of you who aren't familiar with this sixties television classic, it revolves around the life of a widowed sheriff, Andy, and his son, Opie. They live in the small town of Mayberry.

In this particular episode, Andy asked Miss Ellie, the single female pharmacist, to the local church picnic. However, somewhere between asking Miss Ellie to the picnic and telling his family back home about the event, Andy confused the details of the story. By the time he was finished telling his tale, Andy was convinced that he was trapped into the date by a designing female who wanted to marry him.

It wasn't long until Opie came home with a vanilla ice cream cone, which he received as a gift from the single female pharmacist.

Well, that sealed the deal!

Andy was sure that Miss Ellie was nothing more than a desperate female hunter who needed to be stopped. On and on he went about the dangers of the desperate female hunter who is trying to trap a man. Unfortunately for Andy, he didn't stop thinking about how great of a catch he was in time to realize that two very little ears were absorbing every word.

The next scene opens up at the pharmacy, where Opie went to purchase another ice cream cone. Of course, this time Opie is very explicit that he will be paying for the ice cream himself, because he's not allowed to take anymore free ice cream cones.

Smiling at the adorable little boy in front of her, Miss Ellie asks, "Why not?"

Opie responds, "My Pa says that ice cream you gave me was the down payment on a husband."

A stunned Miss Ellie laughs and says, "He said what?"

Opie stands by his story and says, "My Pa says that ice cream you gave me was the down payment on a husband. My Pa says that a female who would bait a trap with a fellow's own son was a desperate female hunter. And there ain't but one way for the quarry to outfox the hunter—to put her on the scent of other game."

By this time Miss Ellie is very annoyed and insulted at Andy. That's when Opie innocently asks, "Are you a desperate hunter, Miss Ellie? 'Cause I know where you can get yourself a possum."

I love this episode and Opie's sheer innocence! Of course, Miss Ellie was not a desperate female hunter and she was not trying to trap Andy into anything—as she goes on to prove throughout the show. She was just a kind, single working girl trying to be nice to a little boy.

So where would Andy get such a crazy idea? Well, it could have been his inflated ego or it could have been previous experiences with women who were desperate female hunters.

Let's be honest, we all know they are out there. We've all known women who are so desperate for love that they will go to any extreme to trap a man—any man. These women go beyond the natural, God-given desire placed inside of women to be married. For the desperate hunter, finding a partner has become an obsession. They will go to any lengths, including desperate measures, to get what they want.

In this chapter, we are going to address the choice to avoid being a desperate female hunter. Let's say it's a Christian woman's guide to dating.

Unfortunately, we live in a society full of desperate female hunters who have abandoned biblical standards concerning dating and relationships. However, God has not changed his standards, and it is time that Christians reestablish the biblical boundaries and become a light in a dark world.

So, let's get started. How can we tell the difference between a godly woman and a desperate female hunter? Let's continue with Opie's analogy and look at the differences between a sportsman and a desperate hunter in nature.

I grew up in rural Pennsylvania. Hunting is a BIG deal here. Personally, I don't get the thrill. I have no idea why anyone would want to get up at four o'clock in the morning, get dressed in a hideous orange costume that has been sitting in the attic or basement for the last twelve months, and go out in the freezing cold to climb a mountain and wait to shoot a poor defenseless animal. This does not sound like a good time to me. My idea of the perfect hunt is going to the department store and finding the perfect dress in my size at 50 percent off plus an additional coupon. Now that's a hunt I can understand and enjoy!

Still, no matter how ridiculous it seems to me, every year most of the men (and a few ladies) in my area will trek out into the wilderness in search of their prize. Growing up in this area, I've picked up a little knowledge of the sport. One thing I know is that there are very specific rules and guidelines that each hunter must follow. The same is true of Christian dating and finding a husband. God has established specific boundaries that we should not cross. When we break his laws, we have entered into the territory of becoming a desperate hunter. Here are a few of the laws we need to keep:

- **desperate hunters ignore NO TRESPASSING signs** •

When I was growing up, our family home was at the base of a mountain. Behind our home was a wooded area where deer loved to roam. Because this was private property and it was so close to houses, NO TRESPASSING signs were posted throughout this area. No one was supposed to hunt here. After all, it was dangerous to shoot this close to houses—someone could get hurt.

There were always some hunters who would not obey this rule. Frequently, we could see hunters and hear them shooting far too close to the houses. Why were they willing to break this rule and put people in danger? They were desperate to catch their prize, and these woods were filled with deer. To get what they wanted, they would go anywhere and break any rule—it didn't matter if anyone got hurt.

Unfortunately, we live in a society where many women break the NO TRESPASSING rule when looking for a relationship. However, it's time that Christian women reestablish the standard and stay away from married men. When a man is wearing a wedding ring, he is completely off limits. A Christian woman should not even flirt with a married man. No exceptions.

The Bible is very clear about this rule. Exodus 20:14 "You shall not commit adultery." As soon as you find out that a man is married, you need to view him as another woman's property. He is not available; he belongs to someone else. Respect that boundary and stay away.

In 1 Timothy 5, Paul gives Timothy specific instructions for how he should interact with the other believers in the church.

Treat younger men as brothers, older women as mothers, and younger women as sisters, with absolute purity.

As Christian women, we need to apply these standards to our relationships with the men in the body of Christ—especially married men. We should treat older married men as if they were our fathers and younger married men as if they were our brothers. We should love our sisters in Christ so much that we would never think of trying to steal their husbands.

I'm sure many of you are reading this and saying, "Adessa, this is such an obvious point. Why bother making it?"

Sadly, many women have allowed their standards to be lowered by the world's influence, and they have resorted to desperate measures to find someone to love them.

Recently, my brother told me a story he heard at a men's retreat. The speaker was talking to the men about purity. As an example, he told how he frequently receives nude and inappropriate photographs and invitations from women in his church, which he immediately gives to his wife to handle.

I have to admit I was so disappointed in my gender. Why would a woman who calls herself a Christian be making such an obvious play for a married man of God?

Ladies, this is wrong. It doesn't matter how lonely you are or how much you want to be married, it is sin to try to trap your brother in Christ into adultery. It is time for Christian women to reestablish the biblical, moral standard that married men are private property—NO TRESPASSING.

• desperate hunters don't dress for safety •

I know from years of watching my dad hunt that proper safety attire is necessary before you go into the woods. All hunters must wear certain colors so that no one gets shot accidentally. Most hunters follow these rules. However, there are always the rogue hunters who won't dress for safety. Instead they wear whatever they feel like wearing and they don't care who gets hurt. Their choice is a disaster waiting to happen.

The same is true for the desperate female hunter who refuses to obey basic biblical principles regarding her attire. These women refuse to dress for the safety of all involved. Instead, they use their sensuality as a trap for men.

This is wrong. Again, this is the result of allowing worldly standards to influence our thinking rather than following the biblical standards of purity.

This is probably the biggest way that society has infiltrated the minds of Christian women. Society tells single women how they need to look and dress in order to find a man. The most commonly used word is *sexy*.

We need to look sexy.

We need to dress sexy.

Our hairstyle needs to be sexy.

Our shoes need to be sexy.

We need to wear pants that make our backside look sexy.

Tops need to be as revealing and sexy as possible.

Advertisements tell us that we even need to smell sexy. Our world presents an image that all men want is sex, so if you want to get married and have a family, you had better become sexy.

Personally, I find it ironic that in a society that claims to be *liberal* and *feminist*, it is the Bible that actually has more respect for women. In God's kingdom, a woman's value isn't determined by her appearance or her sex appeal. Rather, a woman is valuable because she is a human being created in the image of God. Because God loves you, he wants you to excel in every area of your life—physically, mentally, emotionally, and spiritually. He appreciates your skills, talents, and abilities. He is constantly working in your life to make you the strongest, most capable woman you can be.

This is how a man that loves God and sees women through God's eyes will view women as well. He will not be attracted to a woman based on her sexiness. Rather, he will be looking for a partner to share his life. He will not simply be attracted to your physical qualities, but he will be attracted to your commitment to God, your abilities, and your personality.

If this is the type of man you want to attract and marry, then there is no need for you to follow the culture's demand for you to present yourself in a sexy manner. Instead, you have the freedom to obey the Bible and dress modestly and appropriately for your age, body type, and situation. You are free to obey 1 Timothy 2:9-10 which reads,

> *I also want the women to dress modestly, with decency and propriety, adorning themselves, not with elaborate hairstyles or gold or pearls or expensive clothes, but with good deeds, appropriate for women who profess to worship God.*

Now before anyone freaks out, let me say that I am not going to give you a lecture on what not to wear, nor will I to say that Christian women should not dress in the most attractive manner possible. I will not give a list of dos and don'ts or make a judgment about your choices.

Honestly, I don't think I need to do this. I believe, inside, every woman knows the difference between an outfit that makes us feel beautiful and self-confident and an outfit that makes us feel sexy. As Christian women we need to make the conscious choice to choose to wear things that make us feel good about ourselves and avoid wearing things that actually degrade us.

As we're shopping we need to ask ourselves, "Does this outfit tell the world that I am a strong, confident Christian woman? Am I presenting myself to the world as a woman with high standards of purity? Is there anyone or anywhere I would feel uncomfortable or immodest wearing this outfit? As a single woman, what type of man will this outfit attract?"

I started thinking about this the other day when I ran into a single Christian gentleman I knew from years ago. It was a summer day and I was running errands. I had on knee-length walking shorts and a colorful short-sleeved top. This outfit was modest, yet attractive, and made me feel really good about myself. As I walked away I thought, "I'm really glad I looked nice today." After all, who wants to leave a bad impression? On the other hand, I was glad that my outfit was modest and appropriate because I know that he is a godly man and I wanted him to see me as a godly woman.

Honestly, it isn't about a certain type of clothing you should or shouldn't wear—it's about how you present yourself to the world. What does your appearance say about you? Are you saying, "I value myself as a daughter of God" or "I am looking for a man—any man?" Are you willing to commit yourself to rejecting the world's image of the single woman and embracing God's design for your life?

• desperate hunters hunt out of season •

All hunters know that you can't go hunting anytime you want. You can only go hunting during hunting season. Of course, there are always those who hunt out of season even though it is illegal. If they get caught, they could be arrested, but they don't care. They want what they want WHEN they want it.

Recently, I've noticed a trend with single people hunting out of season. Because they are so desperate to find what is missing in their lives, they begin hunting in a season of their lives that has passed. Nostalgia sets in and the desperate female hunter begins thinking, "How could I have let him go?"

Soon they are online searching social networking sites for the one that got away. With just a click of the mouse, we can reconnect and pick up where we left off, hoping to live happily ever after.

Before you hit SEND, there are some dangers of which you need to beware. There is the distinct possibility that the person on the other end may be married. If he is—do not contact him. You are entering a NO TRESPASSING ZONE.

You may ask, "Why not? I'd just be looking up an old friend."

Even if that were true, it's still not a good idea. Why?

Think about what you remember about the other person. What does he look like? Are you imagining a person in his thirties, forties, fifties, or are you picturing him the way he was when you knew him?

The same thing is true for him. If you contact him, he will immediately remember you the way you were when he knew you. You will be resurrecting memories of fun times, young romantic love, and carefree dreams. As he is having all these memories, he may begin to compare his wife, who is waiting for him to talk about the budget and take out the trash, with the memory of a carefree, young girl. As he begins to play the "would have, could have, should have" game in his head, you could be responsible for serious damage to his current life and relationships.

Destroying someone else's life isn't caring about that person. It's being selfish and it shows signs of desperation. So let the past stay in the past. That season is over, and the decisions that were made cannot be changed.

Here's another reason to refrain from returning to a season that has passed: very often, nostalgia has selective memory. As we reflect on former loves and years gone by we tend to concentrate only on the happy, warm, fuzzy memories. We remember a stroll in the park or holding hands under the moonlight. Nostalgia completely blocks out the memory of feeling oppressed by his demanding personality or his tendency toward laziness.

Recently, I heard the story of a woman who reconnected with a man she considered marrying. She chose to reconnect because she remembered all the romantic ambitions and dreams they had together. However, it only took a few dates until she remembered why she ended the relationship in the first place. She couldn't believe that she wanted to go back there!

Going backward is dangerous. You made your life decisions for a reason. Don't let loneliness cause you to reconsider your decisions and make new, desperate decisions. Leave the past in the past and choose to live in this season in your life. Who knows what wonderful things God has planned for your future? Don't give in to desperation—give God a chance to work in this season of your life.

• desperate hunters do not heed warning signs •

DANGER! BEWARE! ROUGH TERRAIN AHEAD!

Warning signs are always posted for a reason. If you ignore them, you will encounter danger. If you heed them, you will avoid trouble.

The same is true for single women. Unfortunately, the desperate female hunter refuses to see the warning signs and retreat. She will not listen to friends or family members who try to warn her of problems with the man of her choice. Though they are genuinely trying to help her, she dismisses their warnings and heads right into trouble.

Here are some examples:

Warning sign: People keep telling you that he has a history of abusing the people in his life.

The desperate female hunter says, "He's changed. I'm sure it won't be that way with me."

Warning sign: He has two ex-wives who agree that he's a lying, cheating scoundrel.

Desperate female hunter says, "Witches—both of them. They were horrible women who just didn't know how to treat him. He's not the problem, they are."

Warning sign: Your parents and sisters tell you that they don't like the way he treats you. This is not a healthy relationship.

Desperate female hunter says, "You just don't want me to be happy. You want me to be alone my whole life."

Are you getting the picture? Warnings were meant to be heeded. At the very least, they should cause you to slow down and proceed with caution. Don't be so desperate to be with someone that you ignore warnings and walk right into danger.

• **desperate hunters will take any lame, sick animal that comes along** •

On the first day of hunting season, all the sportsmen dream of getting the biggest deer with the biggest rack. (Seriously, whoever gets the deer with the biggest horns on their head wins. Silly, I know.)

As the season goes on, the hunters' expectations lower.

They don't need a big buck, just a buck.

If they don't get a buck, they go for a doe.

By the very end of the season, the desperate hunters will take anything they can get.

Unfortunately, the same is true for the desperate female hunter. She will take any man just to get a man. Ladies, this is not God's will for his daughters. He does not want you to become so obsessed in your search for a husband that you lower your standards and settle for an ungodly man who doesn't treat you well.

This is not just true for adults. The sad thing about this point is that we have young girls of thirteen, fourteen, and fifteen who are already so desperate for a boyfriend that they will settle for any boy they can get and they will allow him to treat them very badly just so they aren't alone.

The reality of the desperate female hunter has nothing to do with a woman's age. It is a heart problem. It is the feeling inside that you aren't worth anything unless you are in a relationship. There are unmet needs inside your soul that are desperately crying out to be filled. These needs are causing you to do whatever you need to do to find someone to love you. That's why you are willing to settle for someone that you know doesn't treat you right, isn't good for you, and won't provide you with a healthy, stable life.

You may be reading this chapter and saying, "I never realized it before, but I am a desperate hunter. What can I do?"

Well, the first thing I suggest is that you take a season off.

Take some time and stop dating and looking for a relationship. During this season, take the time to find out why you are this way. Matthew 6:33 says, "But seek first his kingdom and his righteousness, and all these things will be given to you as well."

As Christians, our first calling is to seek his kingdom and his righteousness. This includes asking Jesus to heal the broken things inside of you and make them whole and healthy.

What can you do to seek his kingdom and his righteousness?

Start with prayer.

Ask the Holy Spirit to show you why you have become a desperate hunter.

Are there hurts from your past that need to be healed?

Have prior relationships left you broken and scarred?

Is there sin in your life that is keeping you from being able to see yourself as God sees you?

God knows your heart better than you do. As you spend time in prayer, he will show you why you make the choices you do. As he heals your heart, he will help you to make better choices.

Another benefit from spending time in prayer is that your relationship with God will be strengthened. You will get to know him better. As you experience his love, many of the needs in your heart will be filled. When you are ready to date again, your standards will be much higher because, having experienced God's love, you will find it difficult to settle for less.

Something else you may want to consider is the possibility that your tendency to be a desperate female hunter may be generational.

Maybe great-great Grandma had an experience in her life that traumatized her ability to have healthy relationships and scarred her self-image. It is possible that she passed her unhealthy attitudes and beliefs about relationships on to her daughter, who passed them down to Grandma, who passed them on to Mom, then to you. It may be a generational pattern that needs to be broken by the power of the Holy Spirit.

How do you do this? Start by recognizing the root of the problem. Really look at your ancestors, their experiences, their attitudes, and their behavioral patterns. Ask the Holy Spirit to show you any patterns of low self esteem, self-abuse, signs of desperation or a willingness to accept abuse. Be willing to see the truth so that you can make the determination to overcome.

After you recognize the pattern, choose to forgive your family for accepting these unhealthy mindsets and making sinful choices. Then ask God to forgive you for following in their footsteps and walking in their ways rather than God's ways. Finally, pray that God will set you free from each and every generational iniquity that is keeping you in bondage. Ask God to help you see yourself and your value through his eyes, and not the distorted vision of wounded generations that have gone before.

If you can't work through this on your own, you may want to seek the help of a pastor or Christian counselor who can help you break the cycle. Just because you inherited great-great Grandma's issues, doesn't mean they have to control your life. You can choose to overcome generational iniquities and start a new legacy of daughters who aren't desperate hunters.

You might be saying, "Okay, I've taken time and worked through my issues. I don't want to be a desperate hunter anymore. However, I still want to get married and have a family."

Of course you do. This is a natural God-given desire placed inside of all women. It's not wrong. So here's my suggestion—**change sports. Instead of hunting, try fishing.**

What's the difference?

Hunters go out and spend their time tracking their game until it's captured. On the other hand, fishermen bait their hooks, throw their lines in the water and wait for the fish to come to them. This is a good example for Christian women to follow. Live your life. Enjoy your life and the people in it. Become the best person that you can be. When it is time for you to meet someone, God will arrange it.

Another thing about fisherman—if they catch a fish and it doesn't meet their standards, they throw it back and wait for the next fish! This is a great principle for moms to teach their daughters. Keep your standards high and don't settle for anyone who isn't fully committed to loving God, obeying his commandments, and treating his daughters with the proper respect. If you are following these standards, no one will ever be able to call you a desperate female hunter.

• • ● • •

Dear heavenly Father, I know that this chapter tried to approach a difficult topic from a humorous perspective, but I have to admit that there were times when some of the analogies convicted my heart. You and I both know that there have been times when I've acted like a desperate female hunter. Father, I ask you to forgive me.

Today, I ask that you would help me to change. Please help me to hold myself to a higher standard and be willing to wait for a gentleman who is fully committed to loving you, obeying your commands, and treating me and my family with love and respect. I want the best you have for me. God, please help me to wait on you and resist the urge to ever be a desperate female hunter again. In Jesus' name, amen.

• the next step •

1. what comes to your mind when you hear the phrase "desperate female hunter"? how do you relate to this phrase? what past actions would qualify you to have this title?

2. how can we avoid NO TRESPASSING signs?

3. how can a woman present herself as confident and attractive while still dressing for safety?

4. what decisions from your past do you regret?

5. how can we overcome the pull of nostalgia?

6. what warning signs do you tend to ignore?

7. we talked about the differences between hunters and fishermen. how do you feel about following the example of a fisherman?

8. will you choose to NEVER be a desperate female hunter? what changes do you need to make so that you don't fall into this category?

chapter 14 • adessa

choosing purity

"If you love Jesus, should you be having sex outside of marriage?"

The question was posed on social media by a very godly women's minister in an effort to start a discussion. Before long, the comments were rolling in.

At first, the question seems like a no-brainer. "No—the Bible says that sex outside of marriage is sin."

However, for the vast majority of Christian singles, this question isn't so cut and dry. In February 2014, Christianpost.com issued these statistics:

Sixty-one percent of self-identified Christian singles who answered a recent *ChristianMingle* survey said they are willing to have casual sex without being in love.

In a survey of 716 Christians released in January, only 11 percent said they save sex exclusively for marriage. Instead, 60 percent said they would be willing to have sex without any strings attached, while 23 percent said they would have to be "in love."

Five percent said they would wait to get engaged.

This data supports a 2011 *Relevant Magazine* poll that revealed that 80 percent of "young, unmarried Christians have had sex" and that "two-thirds have been sexually active in the last year."

Of course, for most of us, statistics aren't necessary. All we have to do is look around our churches, our women's groups, and our youth groups and realize that Christian's attitudes toward sex outside of marriage have changed to mimic the culture's views that premarital sex is not only not a sin, but it is natural, normal, and totally acceptable.

That's what makes this Christian leader's question not only relevant, but necessary.

You see, as Christians we've been skirting around the issue for too long. Too many leaders, parents, and even singles have been turning a blind eye to the topic of sex outside of marriage rather than facing the topic head on and telling people the truth. In an effort to avoid offending people, we're lying and pretending that sex outside of marriage is no big deal.

The only problem is that according to the Bible, sex outside of marriage isn't just a big deal; it's sin. No matter what the world says or how society wants to change the church's views, the Bible remains the same. As a minister who wants to see women grow spiritually and reach their full potential in Christ, I believe it's time that we stop avoiding the issue and tackle it head on.

Let's start with I Thessalonians 4:3–8, which reads:

It is God's will that you should be sanctified: that you should avoid sexual immorality; that each of you should learn to control your own body in a way that is holy and honorable, not in passionate lust like the pagans, who do not know God; and that in this matter no one should wrong or take advantage of a brother or sister. The Lord will punish all those who commit such sins, as we told you and warned you before. For God did not call us to be impure, but to live a holy life. Therefore, anyone who rejects this instruction does not reject a human being but God, the very God who gives you his Holy Spirit.

If we go back and look at this verse line by line, we see that there are some powerful statements concerning sex outside of marriage.

- **God wants his children to have a different view of sex than society's views on sex** -

Look at the way the English Standard Version translates verses 3–5:

For this is the will of God, your sanctification: that you abstain from sexual immorality; that each one of you know how to control his own body in holiness and honor, not in the passion of lust like the Gentiles who do not know God.

Clearly, it is God's will that his people be different from the world. After all, that's what sanctification means, "being set apart for a holy purpose."

This is what sets the Christian single apart from the non-Christian single: As Christians we accept the fact that we no longer belong to ourselves. We have been bought with the price of Christ's precious blood. Now every part of our lives belongs to God. Our new purpose in life is to complete the mission God has for us in his kingdom.

1 Corinthians 6:19-20 (ESV) puts it this way:

Do you not know that your body is a temple of the Holy Spirit within you, whom you have from God? You are not your own, for you were bought with a price. So glorify God in your body.

So what does all this mean?

When you became a Christian, you agreed that you belonged to God. No part of your life—including your body and your sex life—belongs to you anymore.

It is God's will that you exhibit that you belong to him by living a sexually pure life, that you learn self-control, and that you abstain from the culture of passion and lust that is so common in the world around us. No matter how different or even "freakish" the Bible's commands about sex may see to our modern day society, if we claim to be followers of God and love Jesus, then we are called to be different and live holy lives of sexual purity.

- **God, not man, commands unmarried people to abstain from sex outside of marriage** •

One of the biggest lies commonly accepted among Christian singles today is the idea that God has nothing to say about their sex life. The rules and restrictions about sex outside of marriage are just man-made rules enforced by legalistic Christians.

> *For God did not call us to be impure, but to live a holy life. Therefore, anyone who rejects this instruction does not reject a human being but God, the very God who gives you his Holy Spirit (1 Thessalonians 4:7–8).*

This brings us back to the original question: "If you love Jesus, should you be having sex outside of marriage?"

Well, if you say that you love someone, doesn't it follow that you'd want to show your love by doing the things that please him? I mean, every time I've even just had a crush on someone, I've wanted to do the things that would make him happy. In John 14:21, Jesus takes that logic a step further when he says, "Whoever has my commands and keeps them is the one who loves me."

Perhaps that's why so many who want to be sexually active prefer to believe that the biblical view of sex is simply a man-made archaic rule. That way they can blame "legalism" and never acknowledge that when they choose to have sex outside of marriage they are damaging their relationship with God in much the same way that people who commit adultery are damaging their relationship with their spouse. They are choosing to do the wrong thing and sinning against the one (Jesus) with whom they have entered a covenant relationship.

Does the choice to have sex outside of marriage reflect on your love for Jesus?

Hmmm... The answer is the same as asking, "Does the choice to have an affair say anything about the love you have for your spouse?"

Either way, the choice to do the wrong thing will damage the relationship.

Think I'm going too far? Then read 1 Corinthians 6:16–20 (The Message), which says:

> *There's more to sex than mere skin on skin. Sex is as much spiritual mystery as physical fact. As written in Scripture, "The two become one."*
>
> *Since we want to become spiritually one with the Master, we must not pursue the kind of sex that avoids commitment and intimacy, leaving us more lonely than ever—the kind of sex that can never "become one."*
>
> *There is a sense in which sexual sins are different from all others. In sexual sin we violate the sacredness of our own bodies, these bodies that were made for God-given and God-modeled love, for "becoming one" with another. Or didn't you realize that your body is a sacred place, the place of the Holy Spirit? Don't you see that you can't live however you please, squandering what God paid such a high price for? The physical part of you is not some piece of property belonging to the spiritual part of you. God owns the whole works. So let people see God in and through your body.*

The choice to have sex outside of marriage will have a negative impact on your relationship with God. Ultimately, the choice to completely ignore God's laws and live a promiscuous lifestyle could destroy your relationship with God. This brings us to point number three:

- **those who choose to have sex outside of marriage will not inherit the kingdom of God** •

Galatians 5:19–21 (KJV) explicitly says,

Now the works of the flesh are manifest, which are these: adultery, fornication, uncleanness, lasciviousness, idolatry, witchcraft, hatred, variance, emulations, wrath, strife, seditions, heresies, envying, murders, drunkenness, revelings, and such like: of the which I tell you before, as I have also told you in time past, that they which do such things shall not inherit the kingdom of God.

What is *fornication*? The dictionary definition of fornication is "Sexual intercourse between partners who are not married to each other."

These are the rules of the kingdom that everyone must follow. There are no exceptions. It doesn't matter what society says is okay. If we want to fulfill God's kingdom purpose in our lives now, and be welcomed into the kingdom of God when we die, we must follow God's laws.

Practically, what does this mean? Simply put, a single woman who claims to be a Christian should not participate in any type of sexual activity. God designed sex to be within the confines of a marital commitment. Only when we make a commitment to obey God's laws on this issue are we fulfilling our calling as God's daughters, living by his kingdom rules.

What do you do if you are a sexually active?

You need to change your lifestyle.

This chapter is not meant to condemn you or discourage you. Rather, it is intended to teach you what God expects from you and encourage you to conform your behavior to his standards. It is never too late to repent and change your behavior. Today you can choose to ask God to forgive you for living a sexually immoral life and choose to stop having sex until you are married. If you are living with a man who is not your husband, than one of you should choose to move out. You may even need to end the relationship if he is not willing to repent and conform to God's standards for living.

Take whatever steps are necessary to realign your life with God's biblical standards. Choose to stop sinning and following the world's behavioral pattern. Rather, choose to make the life changes necessary to follow God's will for your life by obeying his laws regarding sex.

Maybe you are a single woman who is not sexually active. You may be reading this chapter with a yawn and saying, "I've heard it all before. No sex until marriage. Is this all God has to say on the topic of sex and the Christian single?"

The answer is a resounding "NO." This is actually just the beginning. God doesn't call his children to only avoid sexual activity outside of marriage. He has called each of us to live pure and holy lives in an impure and unholy culture.

So that you may become blameless and pure, children of God without fault in a warped and crooked generation. Then you will shine among them like stars in the sky as you hold firmly to the word of life (Philippians 2:15-16).

Can you imagine? In this Scripture, Paul encourages believers to live in such a way that they are a light in the darkness just as the stars stand out in the night sky. This means that our purity needs to be a characteristic that sets us apart from the world and distinguishes us as daughters of God.

But realistically, how can a woman maintain this level of sexual purity?

Let's rephrase that to ask some really honest questions:

How can a teenager commit to saving sex for marriage when it seems like everyone around her is sexually active?

How can a single woman in her twenties, thirties, or even forties or fifties be expected to control her sexual desires and abstain from sex until she's married?

What steps can a woman who's been married and is now single or a woman that's been sexually active in the past take to control her sexual appetites and live as a godly woman?

Are there any practical tips that can help the woman who wants to obey the Bible's commands about sex and the Christian single?

Here are some practical tips to help you choose purity:

• to choose purity, you need to make a commitment to abstinence •

Years ago, we would have called this "having a plan." Whatever we call it now, the fact remains that you can't wait until you're in the passionate heat of the moment to decide whether or not you're going to obey or disobey God's laws. Before you even go out on a date, you need to resolve in your heart that you are wholeheartedly committed to following God's commands for abstinence, and create a plan for how you're going to stick to your commitment.

Part of the plan could be committing to only dating men who have the same commitment or making it clear right from the start of the relationship that you are committed to obeying God's laws regarding sex.

A few years ago, a woman who was single into her thirties shared her testimony with *A Wellrounded Woman Magazine*. During her interview, she told of informing the man she'd been dating for about two weeks that she was committed to waiting until she was married to have sex. Although she was really nervous about his response she thought, "What do I have to lose? I'm not changing my mind, so we might as well deal with it up front."

That night over dinner, she told him that she was committed to waiting until she was married to become physically intimate. He had no problem with waiting and never pushed to do anything she felt was sinful. Today, they are married and have two little boys, and she encourages other young women to follow her example.

Another part of your plan may include setting boundaries as to how far you will become physically involved before you are married, what times of day you feel comfortable being alone with a gentlemen, and even what types of places you feel are suitable for a Christian couple to go to on a date.

Even though setting these types of boundaries ahead of time may seem old-fashioned or antiquated, that's just because we live in a culture that has no boundaries. As Christians, we are called to be counter-culture and live for a higher calling and purpose—glorifying God with our bodies and fulfilling his purpose for our lives. Meeting this goal isn't going to just happen—a Christian single woman is going to have to put thought, effort, and resolve into making a commitment to purity and taking the steps to keep that commitment.

- **to choose purity, you should have someone in your life that will hold you accountable** •

Accountability is a powerful tool. Having a friend or an older woman who serves as a mentor, encouraging you to keep your commitment to sexual purity will be a tremendous asset in the life of any single. Giving her the freedom to ask any question at any stage of the relationship will help you keep your commitment to sexual purity.

Why?

Well, because she isn't swept up in the emotions, the romance, and the desire of the moment, she can help keep you grounded in reality. She will remind you of your commitment to God and purity before you do something you will regret. She'll help you stick to your pre-established boundaries and remind you that true love waits, helping you avoid sin and develop a strong, healthy relationship with the person you're dating.

Two are better than one, because they have a good return for their labor: If either of them falls down, one can help the other up. But pity anyone who falls and has no one to help them up.... Though one may be overpowered, two can defend themselves. A cord of three strands is not quickly broken (Ecclesiastes 4:9–12).

Which brings us to point number three:

- **to choose purity you must focus on your relationship with God**

I've said it before and I'll probably say it again: one of the most annoying phrases to hear as a single woman is "Make Jesus Your Boyfriend."

It always sounds so lame. That's when my snarky, sarcastic side would come out and I'd think, "Yes, that will fix everything, won't it?" and then I'd go off on some mental rant about condescending couples not having a clue about what it's really like to be single. (Was that a little too honest and vulnerable?)

So, obviously, that's not where I'm going with this.

What I am saying is this: As you invest in your relationship with Jesus, you'll find that he will fill many of the needs in your soul that the world seeks to fill through casual sex.

Let me explain: Recently, I was watching a rerun of one of my favorite television shows about a single woman. Even though I like the show and I do believe it presents the main character as a strong, competent, vibrant, single woman,

I've been noticing an on-going pattern in the storyline that bothers me.

The cycle is this: Every time the main character has an emotional crisis, feels insecure, or is faced with a painful issue from her past, she has casual sex with whatever man is in her life at the time. In the end, these relationships never work out because she doesn't love the man she's sleeping with, nor does she really want a commitment. What she wants is to use sex as a way to stop the pain in her soul. Of course, in the end, she just ends up with more pain as she endures the consequences of the unplanned, uncommitted sexual encounter.

Even though this is just a television show, fiction is imitating real life for far too many women in America—even women in the church. There are needs in their hearts and souls that aren't being met, so they seek temporary solace in a relationship and casual sex in an attempt to fill those needs. Of course, this is only a temporary solution, causing women to go from relationship to relationship rather than ever dealing with the issues in their hearts. In the end, they are only compounding their heartache and adding to their emotional baggage because sex was never designed to be a cure for the wounds of the human heart. Only Jesus can do that.

That's why it's important that all women focus on building a strong relationship with Jesus. There's no better way to learn who you are, who you were designed to be, and what you were meant to accomplish than by spending time with the one who created you. As you spend time with Jesus, he will begin the process of healing the wounds from your past.

As these wounds are healed, you will become a stronger, healthier person spiritually, emotionally, and mentally.

As you spend time in his Word, the Holy Spirit will begin removing any misconceptions and illogical thinking that is playing games with your mind and keeping you from living in spiritual, emotional, and mental freedom. The more you saturate your mind with the Word of God, the more it will guide your thinking, helping you to see and understand truth. This will help you relate to God, yourself, and other people better.

Truly, as you develop your relationship with Jesus and allow him to heal your soul and fill the needs of your heart and mind, you'll find that you really have no desire for casual sex. Instead, as you learn to see yourself through God's eyes, you'll understand that you deserve nothing less than the fully committed relationship that comes from marriage.

Okay, now on to point number four:

• to choose purity you're going to have to stop feeding your mind sexual images •

Years ago when I was in Sunday school, we sang a song that said, "Oh be careful little eyes what you see." Now as an adult I know the value of these words, especially for those of us who are single.

Regardless of our age, we, more than anyone else, need to be careful what we watch and listen to because these things will influence the way we feel, the way we see ourselves, the things we desire, and the choices we make. As emotional beings, we are influenced by media. That's why we have to be choosy about the media we let influence us.

Romantic storylines are especially dangerous for women because as we get into the plot we tend to become emotionally involved. We laugh at the heroine's blunders and we cry as she endures her struggles. We watch the romance grow between the characters and wait for them to finally realize they are in love. Then, because we want to see the end of the story, we ignore the fact that their romance ends in the bedroom instead of at the wedding altar.

Unless we change the channel or walk out of the movie, this type of entertainment usually results in us filling our minds with images of nudity and passionate sex. (Pornography for women.) Just like all pornography, these images do nothing more than arouse desires that a Christian single woman cannot fulfill. The only cure for this dilemma is to stop filling our minds with this type of entertainment.

This standard applies to reading material. You can't fill your mind with magazine articles and romance novels containing sexually explicit content and expect to keep your mind pure. Sometimes even Christian novelists cross the line and tell stories that are too sexually graphic. Don't read these books. Instead, read books that encourage you in your endeavor towards purity and fill your mind with good thoughts.

Of course, we can't leave out our musical choices. If I'm always listening to music where the lyrics talk about sex and romance, my mind is going to be constantly thinking about sex and romance. Before long, I'll be thinking about the things that are missing from my life, craving them, and allowing my natural desires to control my life.

This progression is exactly why Paul says in Colossians 3:2 says, "Set your minds on things above, not on earthly things." That's why the Christian single woman who is struggling with sexual temptation or even the temptation to be depressed that she is not in a relationship needs to turn off the secular radio, and start listening to Christian music that will build her up and encourage her to continue her quest for purity.

At our house (where my brother and I are both Christian singles), we have established certain guidelines for our entertainment choices, specifically our television viewing, that we feel help us maintain a pure lifestyle. (We don't go to the movies.)

First, we set the parental controls on our television to PG with sexual content blocked. This helps eliminate programs with a sexually explicit nature.

Secondly, we avoid all sex scenes. Years ago, my pastor's wife, Devi Titus, taught us that whenever you watch a couple in bed together you are watching pornography. Her teaching has become a rule at our house. Whenever a program turns toward a bedroom scene, we turn it off. We do not need those images replaying in our minds.

Thirdly, if we accidentally come across a program with a sexually explicit topic or unnecessarily crude language, we immediately change the channel. This is the power that will help you keep your mind pure: You have the responsibility to stop watching or listening to entertainment that does not follow the guidelines of Philippians 4:8.

As you stop filling your mind with these images and messages, you will stop being influenced by the world's thinking. Your conscience will stop being desensitized to accept sin and it will start becoming sensitive to the conviction of the Holy Spirit. Most importantly, when you stop feeding your mind sexual images, you'll see a significant decrease in your sexual appetite and desires.

Here's another thing that we don't often think about:

- **to choose purity, you'll need to avoid sexually explicit conversations** -

How many of us have been with a group of Christian women when someone in the group decides to talk openly about their sexual experiences? Have you ever been with someone who saw a movie or television show that you knew was too racy, yet you allowed them to tell you about it?

The Christian single woman who is committed to obeying the Bible's commands about sex needs to avoid these types of conversations. Why? Because hearing someone tell a graphically sexual story is the same as looking at pornography. Your sexual desires are being aroused, creating the desire inside of you to sin. In both cases, you are filling your mind with sexual images.

Instead, we need to choose to obey the Bible which says in Ephesians 4:29 "Do not let any unwholesome talk come out of your mouths, but only what is helpful for building others up according to their needs, that it may benefit those who listen."

Our conversation should fit the description in Colossians 4:6: "Let your conversation be always full of grace, seasoned with salt, so that you may know how to answer everyone."

So, back to our original question: How can we, as Christian single women, avoid the temptation to sin sexually and stand up against the lies of a culture that promotes the virtues of promiscuous sex at every turn?

It comes down to this: God created sex for marriage and only for marriage. If you are a Christian single woman, then sex is not an option for you at this time in your life. Why, then, would you want to spend all your time talking, thinking, and focusing on something you can't have?

It's like a diabetic working in a bakery or a former alcoholic working at a bar.

By choosing these environments, you're making your life harder and increasing your temptation.

2 Corinthians 6:17 speaks to believers and says, "Therefore, 'Come out from them and be separate, says the Lord.'"

In a world that is dominated by sexual promiscuity and impure living, we as Christian singles need to obey this call and separate ourselves from the culture. As followers of Christ, our lifestyle of purity should set us apart as different from the world around us. It should be our defining characteristic. Because of the way we live our lives, speak to others, and choose to present ourselves, people should be able to identify us as God's daughters following his kingdom principles.

Several years ago, I read a newspaper article about a popular Christian football player. (Granted he's not a woman, but the principle applies.) The reporter asked him the question, "Do you plan to save yourself for marriage?"

The Christian man said, "Yes."

However, it was the next line in the article that stayed with me. The reporter wrote, "I'd have been surprised if he'd given any other answer. We all know he's a Christian and I completely expected him to live by his beliefs."

Could the same be said about you?

If you were chatting over coffee with a friend, would she ask you about your sex life or would she know that you're waiting for marriage?

Do your co-workers expect you to be participating in the same entertainment as they do, or are they aware of your commitment to purity?

Do the off-color conversations become hushed when you're around because people know you're a Christian, or do you laugh along with a dirty joke?

What is your reputation?

At the end of the day, are you choosing purity?

• • • • •

Dear heavenly Father, I come to you today confessing that it is hard to live a pure life in a very impure world. Still, nothing in my life is more important to me than my relationship with you. Because of this I'm choosing to live in purity as a woman of God. Please forgive me for every sexual sin I've committed in my past. (This would be a good time for personal confession.) Please help me to live the rest of my life in purity. Convict me when I am choosing media that is impure, participating in impure conversations, or allowing myself to be influenced by the world. Help me to create a plan to have healthy, godly relationships. Lead me to a godly friend who will hold me accountable to live every part of my life for your glory. Jesus, I love you more than anything else in this world. Please help my actions to demonstrate this as I choose to follow biblical standards for purity. In Jesus' name, amen.

• the next step •

1. the chapter opens with the question: "if you love Jesus, should you be having sex outside of marriage?" what's your answer?

2. do you believe it is possible to obey the bible's standards for purity in a modern world?

3. does sexual impurity have an effect on your relationship with God?

4. what are some proactive steps that you plan to take to maintain purity in your life?

chapter 15 • jennie

choosing purity again

We are called to live a life of righteousness. We are called to obedience. We are called to holiness. As Christians, we should be reflecting all that God has instructed us and admonished us to be. This includes living and acting in purity.

For some sad reason, our society most commonly uses the word *pure*, these days, to describe and market our food, but will rarely, if ever, encourage us to live our lives this way. On the contrary, more people seem to be shocked to hear of someone who has chosen to live a life of purity and most specifically, sexual purity.

Before I was married, I remember being scrutinized and borderline interrogated at doctors' offices when they asked if I could be pregnant and I explained that I was a virgin. They just couldn't comprehend that someone would save sex for the sanctity of marriage. They also couldn't understand how one could have the willpower to do so. Occasionally, I would get a response of, "Aww, that's so sweet." Really?! It isn't just sweet, it's biblical! It is written in plain ink. Black and white. No gray on this one, girls! God is clear about our sexual purity and keeping sex for marriage only! There are many examples of this in Scripture as well as the consequences that occur when we don't heed God's instruction for his best in our lives.

When we choose to be a follower of Christ, we identify ourselves as such, and if we are calling ourselves Christians, then our actions and daily choices need to begin to reflect his instruction, the written Word of God. It is a choice to live in obedience; not an easy one, but the concept is simple.

The benefits of choosing to live in sexual purity are invaluable. The less baggage and ties you bring into a marriage, the less drama and issues you will have to overcome. Having sex with someone ties you to them and binds you to them like no other form of intimacy in a relationship. That is how God designed it. He designed it to bind a couple together and unite them as one and in the context of marriage, this gift he's given is a tremendous blessing. Outside of marriage, it becomes a bondage. We become tied to the wrong people, and unfortunately, we carry that bond into every new relationship. It's like trying to run with twenty pounds of ankle weights on. Not impossible, but certainly not easy nor God's best for us.

Okay, now that we are clear that it is not part of God's divine design for our lives, what do you do if you are not exactly able to identify yourself as "The 40-Year-Old Virgin" and you have experienced way more than you care to admit? Or maybe you're in a similar scenario to mine, where you remained sexually pure until you were married, but…your spouse checked out and now you're left to navigate the deficit of physical intimacy. In either situation, there is hope! Purity is possible at this stage of the game.

Ladies, if you want to consecrate yourselves to the Lord and live for him only, then you cannot allow yourselves to be slaves to your physical and emotional desires. You cannot serve two masters! I completely understand hormonal fluctuations and the issues that ensue once you've opened Pandora's box of physical intimacy. But I strongly encourage you to put that mess of a box back down and choose to honor the Lord with all that you are and have in this season of singleness. I promise you that God will bless your obedience! Besides, do you really want a man who is willing to lure you away from the blessings God has for you? Sure, he may look fantastic and smell AMAZING and may even quote Scripture, but is he going to lead your home in the things of God and encourage you to walk closer to the Lord? He is spouting nonsense if he is also trying to lead you to the bedroom!

I apologize if you feel I am coming across a little harsh. It may be due to the effects sexual impurity and lack of consecration to God's will have had on my own marriage. Once you start smudging lines right along with society and you stop adhering to biblical truth, you begin to play a dangerous game. If you catch yourself thinking, "It's just this one time, I know God will forgive me," you are messing with grace. And for the record, grace is something you look back on, not forward to!

If you are choosing today to live rightly and purely for the Lord, God's grace and mercy is right there ready and waiting to embrace you. Your past can be redeemed and all of your sin and the shame it's caused you can be erased in the eyes of God and you can be seen as new and whole.

Today is a new day. It's time to get really stubborn about this topic and not allow anything to sway you from here on out.

Don't put yourself in compromising scenarios where you are alone with a man. If someone could make assumptions of your behaviors based on your talk, your whereabouts, or your actions, avoid those things altogether. No excuses!

Get your thoughts in check with the word of God. If they aren't reflecting Philippians 4:8, then make an adjustment.

Get accountable. Find a girlfriend that you trust and someone who is going to tell you like it is. Be sure it's someone you can be transparent and real with, as well as trust to put you back in line and love you even when you may have failed. A balance of grace and truth are what we are after here.

Make the choice that "under no circumstances will I have sex outside of marriage." I have never given myself even the right to think, "well, maybe…if…" Nope! No ifs, ands, or buts about it. It has to be a conscious daily decision to live in purity. Neither before my marriage, during, or after, have I ever given myself the permission to entertain such thoughts. If the thoughts are ludicrous enough for you to shut down and they are not an option to even think, then the concern for them to become actions will be greatly reduced.

I can only encourage you to live in a way that I have personally found possible and of which I have reaped the benefits. Thank God for the tenacity and will that he has given you (traits that may be viewed as pure stubbornness in other areas). Let them be seen as gifts in this scenario, that as you set your mind on the things of him, you will refuse to waiver in your decision to live in purity.

• • • • • •

Dear Lord, I seek you today for accountability in this area of sexual purity. I understand that this begins in my mind and I am choosing to surrender my thoughts to you. I am sorry for the times that I have stepped away from your best for me and have sinned against you. Please help me to walk in purity and in truth. I commit my sexuality to you and I am making the choice, from this moment forward, to walk in purity as you've instructed me to. Help me to reach out to others that will keep me accountable, as well as to make necessary changes in my life that will make it possible to remain pure. I thank you for your grace and instruction. In Jesus' name, amen.

• the next step •

1. in the past, in what areas have you allowed yourself to cross the line of purity? in relationships? movies? internet? books or magazines?

2. what changes do you need to make that will help you to be more successful at walking in purity?

3. who is someone you feel can help keep you accountable in this area?

4. make a verbal declaration to someone that you are going to choose today to honor God in the area of sexual purity.

chapter 16 • jennie

choosing to live for a single purpose

*T*wo and a half years ago, my seemingly happy marriage and home were abruptly shattered when my husband of ten years disclosed that he had been having an affair with a woman in our church. Despite my willingness to move toward healing and restoration of our marriage, he was not, and subsequently he chose to move in with a whole new family and other children apart from his own. Two marriages and families were torn apart because of these decisions.

Because of how well known the situation was in our church and our community, I felt it necessary to move out of our town and in with my parents to have a safe haven for my daughter, Tali, and I to heal. We lost our beautiful historic home, some friends, and our sense of security. I packed and sold items in our home in a flurry and tried to evacuate as quickly as possible. We suddenly had no steady income or provision as my child support didn't start coming till my divorce finalized a year and a half later and my once kind, generous, loving, and supportive husband was no more.

I never thought I'd be walking in such heavy, clunky, painful shoes that were adorned with rejection, pain, betrayal, insecurity, and grief—but suddenly, there I stood. I was angry, hurt, and so broken. I remember falling to my knees in my empty home and screaming to the Lord, "What do I do now?!" He didn't necessarily give me an answer as to what was going to unfold before me in the coming days or months. Honestly, I don't know that I could've handled knowing. But he did flood me with the grace and strength to get up off the floor and pack another box. Then, to make one decision after another as they arose. With each one, I was able to respond with wisdom and truth and grace beyond my own capacity, especially in those weak moments.

Many, many times the weight of life and emotion and stress was so heavy that I physically could not take another step, and I'd lay on the floor of my room and sob. Each of those times, and many in between, I handed every moment, decision, hurt, anger, and grief over to God and let it go. I surrendered what I thought I knew, how I wanted to respond, and released my anger and how I thought things should go. I let go of all of me. I was willing to even look at what in me needed to change and what God could make better in me in my brokenness.

Many parts of me, in the past, remained hidden from God…or so I thought. I was too prideful or embarrassed to bring them before the Lord in my quiet times, and I thought I could keep them looking all neat and tidy enough to manage them. All the while, I wasn't willing to give God all of me and every so often the clutter would pile up in me and become unsightly! I would go through the cycle of genuinely apologizing and then just tidying up my messy self to be presentable again. Interestingly enough, when my whole world crashed and it was way too messy of a job for me to conceal or even try to muddle through on my own, I found that I was able to be completely vulnerable before the Lord and with others.

I was finally willing to let God do what I call "filleting me." Completely open, raw and exposed; all my ugliness before the Lord for us to look at together and for him to cut away. Forgiveness has been a huge part of this process and has literally been a daily task as situations haven't resolved or layers of more pain and hurt have piled on.

I remember taking my grief to the Lord early on and saying, "God, do not waste this pain! I'm willing to do whatever it takes to become better in this process and since I'm already at such a low place, we might as well start here with my brokenness."

We will not be exempt from pain, but we will receive comfort and direction and grace in the middle of it when we surrender our hearts to the Lord.

Often our anger at the Lord for allowing us to walk through such horrific circumstances keeps us from seeing that he's right there to help us and guide us. No matter what is going on around you, keep looking up! Grace is there for us when we need it—in buckets full!

What I realized very quickly is that we can *choose* to walk in grace each day. We can choose to operate in obedience. We can choose to follow the promptings of the Holy Spirit, even when they seem plain crazy! When we make these daily choices, we are lavished with the grace needed to keep walking forward and to combat every fiery dart of the enemy that comes our way.

I've decided that anyone who's ever walked through something traumatizing, hurtful, and devastating has experienced intense anger. Maybe today, you are a little angry! Anger is an emotion that God himself created and, therefore, is completely natural to feel. What we do with it, however, is extremely important as we are responsible for doing what's right even when everyone else is doing wrong. I especially realized my need to be responsible with my anger and responses to my situation when I saw my daughter's big brown eyes staring up at me and watching my every move. It suddenly didn't matter what anyone around me was doing. God made it clear that I was accountable for me and my behaviors.

Ephesians 4:26 says, "In your anger do not sin."

Many situations arose where I found myself needing to say this repeatedly in my head: "Be angry and do not sin, Jennie. Be angry and do not sin." I took my anger and brought it back to God—over and over and over and over. I'd look up and yell "What now?! What are you gonna do now and what am I supposed to do now?" Each time, as I handed that grief and anger back to God, he gave me a grace and a peace to take the next step forward. I wasn't able to see what was ahead until I handed all those raw emotions over to him.

Anger will severely cloud your thoughts and perspective and make it impossible to think rationally and see the beauty before you until you take it back to God and process it before him. Sometimes this is a daily and even moment-by-moment decision and action. But God can handle our emotions, so bring them to him continually.

When I first moved to Georgia last August, we were just getting settled in when I was forced to move again for the fifth time in ten months. It was the craziest of all scenarios that precipitated this move, and it was extremely physically and emotionally stressful. I became overwhelmed with all that I needed to do and how to exit as quickly as possible. It just seemed as if life had thrown me one thing after another that I had to, once again, muddle through. I felt buried under a pile of continual crazy and I threw my hands up in the air and yelled to God, "Now what?!"

At this moment, I knew there was nothing more that I personally could do to fix the problem. I was frantically searching for an apartment with no proof of substantial income, no job, horrible credit, and no down payment. And I needed to get out of this situation we were in immediately.

This was definitely a God-sized problem and I was in such a helpless state that I was finally willing to surrender and let him take over. Again, I needed to hear his voice and get his direction and allow him to step in and do a miracle.

And he did! Within a very short period of time, I was able to find a place that accepted all my issues and restrictions with a simple co-signer and even had a very small deposit due that was available immediately. It didn't come without much work on my part, but I trusted him to lead me and fill in the gaps that I couldn't.

Once I got into the apartment, I faced the fear of not being able to afford the rent each month. Again, I took it back to God and asked, "Now what?" And each time he simply said, "I am your provider." Miracle after miracle, my rent has been paid every month without one bill being paid late.

God will let us keep trying to do and fix and adjust and work through our situations the best way we know how. And often, we keep spiraling and spinning in circles and getting nowhere fast. But the moment we let go of our own plans and ideas of how things should be done and we hand it back over to him, he is able to step in and do exceedingly and abundantly beyond what we could ever imagine. By allowing my daughter to see me trust God and then observe the miracles he's provided, it has slowly rebuilt her faith and trust in him as well.

As I was preparing to write this chapter, I walked into my local Starbucks to spend a much-appreciated gift card and get away from all the distractions at home that would keep me from sitting down and actually getting anything on paper. I'm sure you have no idea what I mean! Etched on the door were the words, "Say YES to what's next!"

Some of you may be reading this thinking, "I don't even know what I'm having for dinner! Jennie, please don't make me think about what plan God has for my life in the midst of my mayhem!" I'm not saying that he will reveal his entire master plan the moment you surrender your days and moments to him, but he will reveal your next step. Sometimes we see a logical solution to our problem and pray that he will work through our situation in the way we think it could best be fixed. What we don't always realize is that he sees the entire picture and knows much better than us.

I thought the solution for me to be able to pay my rent was to get a job—this is entirely logical and highly recommended. However, I was getting nowhere in my search and God kept providing as I trusted him. Not too long into my search, I found out I needed to have surgery and wasn't going to be able to work for a time. All the while, God was faithfully and consistently providing for our needs in the most bizarre and phenomenal ways—complete strangers sending us checks, finding two one-hundred dollar bills in the branches of our Christmas tree, being handed countless gift cards at just the right moment; the list of crazy provision goes on and on.

No matter where you are on your journey with God, you can take time today to let go of the plans you're still holding on to and look to God for the next step he has for you to take. It may seem strange or crazy or unorthodox and usually that's how I know it's his idea and not mine. I am cautious and rational and methodical and logical in all my thinking and planning and reasoning. I know that God is directing me to do something when I am unable to let that idea rest without acting on it and it makes me the most uncomfortable and goes against anything I would ever think of. It may be a job opening for something you feel ill-equipped for or moving to an area that is away from all things familiar or giving to others in need when you are in need yourself. Stepping out in obedience to what God is asking of you is often uncomfortable and inconvenient but when you are obedient to his will, you have such peace when you lay your head to rest at night. We don't have to be good at what God is calling us to do, we just have to be willing and obedient to do it!

Whether you are overwhelmed with grief and anger or just plain frustrated with the happenings of life, I want you to take the opportunity to give it back to God and seek him for the next steps you are to take. Or you may be in a place where the dust has settled, you've got a good rhythm going and life is generally okay, but you wonder what God has for you in this life.

So often we take our list of dreams to the Lord and say, "Please fulfill these ones. These are my dreams and wishes. Make these come true for me." Let's take time to seek God's heart to know *his* dream and plan for our lives and what he wants to do in us right now.

On one of my ugliest and most painful days, I was obedient to write an article for a magazine. I felt so broken, so discarded, and so useless as I sat and stared at my computer screen. I didn't feel as though I had anything left in me to offer anyone else. As I started to type, the words just began to flow and I met the deadline to submit it. I sent it off to the editor with only the assurance that I said what God wanted me to. Nothing more, nothing less.

I was real, honest, and genuine about my pain and losses. I remember shrugging my shoulders and uttering to God, "Well, I did what you asked." Before the article ever made it to print in that magazine, it was submitted to an e-magazine where women from all over the country were reading it and began contacting me. They related to my story. They appreciated my realness and authenticity. From there, I began receiving invitations to speak at various women's events. I was asked to write more and more articles. Every time, I felt the Lord gently nudging me. I knew that what he had written on my heart in the midst of ugly and chaos had prepared me for what he was now launching me into.

Each time I put words on a page, they are coming from a place of brokenness and surrender to the Lord. When I stand before women and share, I can only utter what I've learned in the trenches. My destiny is being created out of my mess. I can only speak from what I've learned. The Bible hasn't been just some sweet, fluffy, encouraging sonnets that I read to boost my morale in those rough times. It has been my lifeline. My TRUTH. I have gleaned wisdom from its pages and the words have become etched on my heart. The peace I gained from genuinely knowing the heart of God is what I am now able to share. You can't effectively teach others until you have experienced and learned and know the truth for yourself.

Try not to get frustrated with small beginnings. It's taking those consistent daily steps in the direction God is leading you that will get you to where you need to be for your destiny and calling to be realized. In my obedience and surrender, I saw God begin to weave a beautiful tapestry out of the rags I kept bringing him. The words he spoke to me in the darkest of moments are the words written in this book. They are the words that he now has me sharing with countless women. I am continually blown away at his ability to use the little I have to offer to reach and minister to other women at just the moment they need it.

Try to enjoy the journey. Even on a rough road, the scenery can be beautiful. Embrace each moment and invite God along for the ride. God can do amazing things with the messy beautiful!

• • • ⬬ • • •

Dear faithful Father, I thank you for your steady grace and provision in our lives. I thank you for carrying us through life's darkest hours and healing us when we are broken. Please help me to seek you always; especially when life is messy and I struggle to see things clearly. Help me to surround myself with others who will speak grace and truth into my life. Today, I choose to seek your plans for my life and to see the beauty that you may be growing from the ashes of my past. You are my truest and most faithful friend and I am grateful for your presence in my life. I love you. You are good and I trust you. In Jesus' precious name, amen.

• the next step •

1. list some times you've already experienced God's protection, provision, or peace.

2. what messy circumstances have you experienced that you can now see God may have a plan for?

3. what areas of your heart and life still need to be surrendered to God?

4. what dreams did you once have, that were maybe displaced or shattered?

5. take some time before the Lord and allow him to speak new dreams into your heart. write down what you feel he is saying to you as you step forward into a whole new season.

conclusion

choices.

In the end, it all boils down to the choices we make. For better or for worse, which road will you take?

After you've read the book, worked through the questions, cried a little, and hopefully laughed a lot, in the end, we hope we've challenged you to make the right choices that will help you live for a single purpose: Seeking Jesus first in your life.

Day by day as you make your choices, we pray that you will understand you are not alone. So many of us are going through the same struggles, working through similar challenges, and making the same choices. Along the way, we're praying for you.

As the apostle Paul prayed in Ephesians 3:16–21 (NLT), this is our prayer for you.

> *I pray that from his glorious, unlimited resources he will empower you with inner strength through his Spirit.*

Then Christ will make his home in your hearts as you trust in him. Your roots will grow down into God's love and keep you strong.

And may you have the power to understand, as all God's people should, how wide, how long, how high, and how deep his love is.

May you experience the love of Christ, though it is too great to understand fully. Then you will be made complete with all the fullness of life and power that comes from God.

Now all glory to God, who is able, through his mighty power at work within us, to accomplish infinitely more than we might ask or think.

Glory to him in the church and in Christ Jesus through all generations forever and ever! Amen.

• ● • ⬤ • ● •

Now go—Choose to live for a single purpose!

about the authors

Adessa Holden is a graduate of the University of Valley Forge and an ordained minister with the Assemblies of God. She is the founder and editor of A Wellrounded Woman Ministries and the co-founder of For a Single Purpose Ministries.

Adessa became a born-again Christian at the age of five, and was raised by a godly mom who taught her and her brother that there was no greater purpose in life than following Jesus. When asked about herself she'll tell you, "I'm a single gal, a woman's minister, a sister, and a daughter. I love to laugh and spend time with friends. I'll eat anything chocolate. I love music, and I'm a bit of a cleaning freak. It is my absolute honor and privilege to serve Jesus Christ and women through this ministry."

Adessa Holden can be contacted at
adessa@awellroundedwoman.com or
adessa@forasinglepurpose.com, where she welcomes any questions, comments, or requests for speaking engagements.

• • ● • •

living for a single purpose

Jennie Puleo considers her most important title to be *mother*; it's always been her dream job. Other titles Jennie currently holds are Registered Nurse, PennDel Women of Purpose Guest Relations Coordinator and co-founder of For a Single Purpose Ministries.

She has always had a deep love for the Lord and her desire to serve and obey him is what has carried her through so many of life's chaotic circumstances. The loss of children, abandonment of spouse, chronic illness, multiple surgeries; so many times and places where God has met her in the middle of a storm! It is now her passion and purpose to share all that God has done in and through her by speaking and writing…and on occasion sharing God's love with that random stranger at a grocery store or in a doctor's office.

She currently lives with her ten-year-old daughter, Natalia, two jet black cats, Ebony and Onyx, and a pup named Mariposa just outside Atlanta, Georgia. Jennie and Tali are often seen exploring historical sites or museums and making their own adventures in the world around them. They both love to travel and, as Jennie's self-proclaimed personal assistant, Tali enjoys traveling with Jennie as she speaks throughout the country. They both have seen God provide for them in miraculous ways over the past three years and are eager to tell others about the goodness of God.

Jennie Puleo can be contacted at **jennie@forasinglepurpose.com** where she welcomes any questions, comments or requests for speaking engagements.

• • ● • •

For more information about For a Single Purpose Ministries and A Wellrounded Woman Ministries, or to see how you can help provide resources to help women grow in their walk with God, contact:

4One Ministries
1109 E. Colliery Avenue
Tower City, PA 17980

Or visit **forasinglepurpose.com** or **awellroundedwoman.com**

ALSO FOR WOMEN

Speaking hope to the hopeless, touching the untouchable, and doing the extraordinary through the ordinary—
JESUS
The Source of Significance.

Finding Significance

Adessa Holden

Founder of *A Wellrounded Woman Ministries*
Cofounder of *For a Single Purpose*

We all crave significance. Adessa Holden's book

FINDING SIGNIFICANCE

will help you understand how God sees you, that he loves to speak hope and new life into those that the world sees as insignificant. Each chapter provides questions for reflection, making it a wonderful tool for self or small group study.

Visit **awellroundedwoman.com** for details.

Also available in both print and digital formats from Amazon, BarnesandNoble.com, and other online retailers.